PR

ON A

BUDGET

Free, Cheap, and *Worth the Money*
Strategies for Getting Noticed

LEONARD SAFFIR

KAPLAN) PUBLISHING

Vice President and Publisher: Maureen McMahon
Editorial Director: Jennifer Farthing
Acquisitions Editor: Karen Murphy
Development Editor: Trey Thoelcke
Production Editor: David Shaw
Typesetter: the dotted i
Cover Designer: Michael Warrell, Design Solutions

Published by Kaplan Publishing,
a division of Kaplan, Inc.

Printed in the United States of America

07 08 09 10 9 8 7 6 5 4 3 2 1

Library of Congress Cataloging-in-Publication Data

Saffir, Leonard.
    PR on a budget / Leonard Saffir.
        p. cm.
    Includes index.
    ISBN-13: 978-1-4195-2367-0 (pbk.)
    1. Public relations.   I. Title.
HM1221.S24 2006
659.2–dc22

                                                        2006020335

DEDICATION

To my wife Eleanor, for putting up with having to listen to my tales of public relations for all our wonderful years together, probably even when I was sleeping.

Contents

Make a note of today's date. If you follow what I say in Chapter 17, *Read, Read, Read,* you will learn over the next 12 months about countless numbers of large companies and small mom-and-pop businesses failing, politicians being soundly defeated, big-time operators going to jail, and good causes going nowhere. And if you could read between the lines, or had the opportunity to ask why, I'll bet you would learn that public relations wasn't a major part of their strategy . . . probably not even a minor part. On the other hand, in the same time frame, you will also read about many success stories, covering the whole gamut, and, for sure, they were driven by a public relations–savvy individual.

When Bill Gates announced at a press conference on June 15, 2006, that he was leaving his day-to-day role at Microsoft to shift his time to philanthropic work, you know that PR professionals orchestrated the press conference, which made the front page of most every newspaper in the country.

I love the craft of public relations. I have helped giant Fortune 100 companies and small businesses, including my own, succeed because of public relations. I have counseled politicians in this country and abroad and helped causes get on the map. It is exciting to write about public relations today because it is an exciting time to be in PR. But you must know that or you wouldn't be reading this book at this time.

I love to hear about success stories, but when I read about a George Bush or Howard Dean doing or saying something without first talking and listening to an experienced public relations practitioner, I could ring their necks. (The truth of the matter is I love it when one of them does screw up, but this book is not about my personal political leanings so I will not divulge whose neck I would wring the strongest.)

Some 25 years ago, between public relations and newspaper jobs, I went into the restaurant business. I was like most people who regularly dream about opening a restaurant and writing a book. I did both and, happily, I had toiled in the vineyards of public relations long enough to call myself a PR professional to help me along the way. Let me tell you one story.

I was sitting with friends in a house one of them had just purchased on a main road in Southampton, New York, one of the fabulous Hamptons. Over drinks, someone said, "This would make a nice restaurant." My friend and I picked up on that and before long we converted the house to a restaurant. Over a Memorial Day weekend—the traditional start of the summer season—we opened a restaurant we called *Carol's* . . . on a tight budget, say credit cards.

Neither of us had ever been in the restaurant business. My friend Carol Rosenwald was an art dealer and I had spent years in PR and journalism.

We decorated the walls with glossy photographs we obtained from photo dealers of celebs named Carol, for example, Carol Burnett, Carol Landis, Carol Bruce, Dianne Carroll, Carol Baker, Barbara Carroll, Carole King, John Carroll, Joyce Carol Oates, Carol Lombard, Lewis Carroll, Caroll O'Connor, J. Caroll Naish, and more. We decided on postage stamp–sized signage out front, so the U.S. Postal Service would know where to deliver the bills. We were going to make it with PR, not advertising. The Carol photos and the lack of signage were part of our strategy.

We hired a man who had recently been fired as head chef at Gracie Mansion, then occupied by New York City Mayor Ed Koch.

In the first few days, our guests included Lee Radziwill (a.k.a. Caroline Lee Bouvier, the sister of Jacqueline Kennedy Onassis) and society scion Gloria Vanderbilt. I proceeded to get items about both in widely read gossip columns written by Liz Smith and Suzy, followed by stories in the local newspapers and Long Island daily, *Newsday,* and the *New York Times.* After all that good PR, one had to call weeks in advance for reservations. The food was excellent but I strongly believe that if all we had was good food and no PR, we would not have succeeded. It is good to have word of mouth going for you, but on a tight budget, one needs faster action. On the other hand, if the food and service are bad, good PR can't help at all.

I left the restaurant business to my partner at the end of the year and went back to my other love, the newspaper business, and subsequently back into PR and one of the largest and best PR firms in the world.

So now let us take a trip through the exciting new age of public relations. Some of this book is about what is happening today, and case histories illustrate the scope, pervasiveness, and power of public relations. At times, you may throw your hands up and shout, "This is not for me. I'm just a small business person." Don't fret. I have included much of how the big guys do things because I feel it is important for everyone to know as much about this giant we call *public relations.*

Some of this book is *how to*—the strategies and tactics that make public relations work. You will read about some new ways PR is practiced today, and you will also learn that today's PR doesn't replace the PR that has been around for decades. It only makes it better and even more challenging.

And I'll tell you a few stories of some experiences of mine, the good and the bad.

For those outside the public relations field or just getting started, this book will help define and explain the new colossus and offer a shortcut to PR literacy.

I would like to thank those who made this book possible.

My agent, Pam Brodowsky, deserves major thanks for believing in me and this book.

Many thanks to Trey Thoelcke and David Shaw of Kaplan for their skillful development and copy editing. As far as I am concerned, they are among the best in the business. Also at Kaplan, my thanks to Karen Murphy and Michael Cunningham for all their help and support from the very first day they heard of the name Leonard Saffir. It takes a village of people to get a book from author to reader.

To my friend Pat Parrish, a one-time editor of mine, and his wife Carolyn, who were the first readers of my draft manuscript, red pencils in hand.

I am particularly indebted to Richard Weiner, a friend and mentor for many years at Richard Weiner, Inc., and then, upon its sale, at Porter Novelli International.

To Robert Dilenschneider, a PR giant, my thanks again for his many contributions.

To William Beecher, a partner in the Dilenschneider Group, for assisting his leader.

Special thanks to my daughter Michelle Saffir, for sharing some of her enormous knowledge of the workings of the Internet with me.

A special thanks to my computer-literate friends Carmen and Bob Berman who were on 24/7 call to respond to my hardware problems.

There are many more who helped, including Jack O'Dwyer, Brian Pittman, Fay Shapiro, Ed Schipul, and Dan Keeney,

Thanks to all the clients I have had the good fortune of working with, who gave me the firsthand knowledge to write this book; and to all the media who, without them, I would not have ever known what great achievement was like.

Thanks to the many PR practitioners I interviewed for this book.

And, lastly, thanks to Sunny, my cockatiel bird, for keeping out of my way (most of the time) while I was writing this book.

Leonard Saffir, one of the luminaries in the public relations world, has written a "how to do it" book expressly aimed at small business people hoping to grasp what PR can do for them on a modest budget, whether they hire a small firm or plan to do it on their own. Young men and women starting out in the PR vineyards as well as old pros will doubtless also find a number of valuable insights.

Saffir has made public relations easy to learn, whether one is a college student, running a small business, fighting for a cause, or even a busy PR illiterate CEO of a large company. And he is happy to share his own successes and failures with candor and a smile, in the hope that others will benefit from his experience.

For Saffir has done it all—working as a foreign correspondent, launching newspapers, big and small, laboring for both one-man and huge PR firms, and serving as the top aide and spokesman for a U.S. senator.

This is a book that only Saffir could write, for he combines his experiences over the years with easy to understand descriptions of all aspects of public relations.

Leonard Saffir is worth listening to and learning from. He is a professional in every sense of the word.

–Robert L. Dilenschneider
Chairman and Founder of the Dilenschneider Group;
former CEO of Hill & Knowlton

1

WHAT IS PUBLIC RELATIONS?

The Engineering of Perception

If you had asked me to define public relations in the years before I entered high school, I couldn't have come up with an answer. Or I might have said something hackneyed like "having relations with the public." Don't laugh. My friend Doug Durrett, from North Carolina, told me about the time he started working for DuPont. As a new employee he got a tour of the boardroom, and one of the guides came from the public relations department. As it happened, the guide was also a DuPont—a member of a family who had by then acquired all the affectations of aristocracy. He told Doug the story of a family reunion where he met an elderly and matronly aunt. Because they had not seen each other for a while, she said, "Jamie, I hear you are with the company now. What are you doing?" He replied that he was in public relations. The shocked aunt said, "Jamie, I understand relations, but public? Really now."

I started practicing PR in my teenage days. After playing schoolyard basketball, I would go home and type up a short story and send it off to my local newspaper. Most always, I got ink, as many PR people refer to getting an item in a publication such as a newspaper or magazine.

Now, after toiling for decades in the vineyards of public relations and journalism, and winning my share of awards in both, I have come up with my own definition of PR.

I call it the *aggressive engineering of perception.*

Perception is reality. We all know that. Some pundits and the media try to demean PR specialists by labeling them as "spin doctors." We (and you, after reading this book) know better.

Perception is the mental image one gets about you, your business, your cause, your quest; even if it is an impossible dream.

Forget about trying to get by today without having a working knowledge of public relations, or not having someone on your team who does.

Take a week in the present-day world. A number of things happen:

- The White House puts a public relations pro in charge of creating a better image for America around the world.
- The president participates in a choreographed video conference call to discuss the situation in a war-torn country.
- A large company, planning to introduce an important new product, entrusts the campaign to the public relations department rather than to the traditional marketing apparatus.
- Public relations practitioners orchestrate a new stock offering by a struggling giant.
- A corporate vice president is recruited to fill a CEO position, substantially on the basis of visibility achieved through PR techniques.
- Facing off in a major lawsuit, the opposing sides hire public relations counsel at the same time they retain legal counsel.
- An online press release generates 100,000 hits the first week it goes online.

- Wal-Mart hires a public relations firm to promote its hurricane relief as part of the overall effort to improve its image.

What's going on here? Has public relations become "The Blob," oozing into every aspect of our lives?

Not quite. But public relations has certainly grown up. Once a kind of corporate office boy, relegated to odd jobs in the communications area, public relations is now a giant, with massive strength and wide versatility.

THE BIRTH OF PUBLIC RELATIONS

Public relations has grown up since the first decade of the 20th century, when Ivy Ledbetter Lee, celebrated as the father of public relations, began to advise various large interests like Bethlehem Steel and the Pennsylvania Railroad.

The railroads, oil companies, steel companies, and utilities had discovered they needed all the image improvement they could get.

Lee's great coup was to have John D. Rockefeller, the epitome of the hard-hearted, tightfisted industrialist, hand out shiny dimes to deserving youngsters. Some big companies today, Halliburton for example, still don't get it. Halliburton has become a dirty name to many in the country, yet I have never seen any attempt on the company's part to correct its image. Had they addressed public relations from the beginning, they could have been on top of the corporate world as a result of their work in Iraq.

A number of brilliant—and sometimes flamboyant—successors to Ivy Lee sold their services to companies throughout the first half of the last century. One of those men was Edward Bernays, a public relations genius who started one of the first PR firms. In 1991—at the age of 100—Bernays was still defending and explaining public relations in our society (he died in 1995).

After World War II, public relations began to become a science—even an art form. More practitioners appeared, larger PR firms were formed, and more companies began to pay serious attention to public relations.

Public relations today affects every aspect of our lives. PR is now a giant, with massive strength and wide versatility. This giant is here to stay. Those who know how to handle it will profit. Those who ignore or mishandle the giant will get hurt, perhaps badly hurt.

Many people still confuse public relations with advertising. In advertising, you pay. With PR, you pray. Advertising professionals sneered at public relations as press agentry compared to their own precise mechanisms. Many in advertising still don't understand public relations, but they don't sneer at it any more. I can't say that about the general public, though.

Harold Burson, the founding chairman of the giant Burson-Marsteller agency and one of the most influential figures in PR, believes PR people don't do a very good job in explaining what they do. "That's why some people consider PR a black art with the purpose to obfuscate, mislead, cover up, or prevent access to corporate executives and public officials. A popular term of derision for what we do is *spin* and we who do the spinning are called *spinmeisters*," Burson says.

The 84-year-old Burson told a Russian PR Association in 2005 that he is "optimistic about the future—yours and, even at my age, mine."

While helping manage the giant Porter Novelli agency in the 1980s, I often said we did an awful job of promoting ourselves. My colleagues reasoned that we couldn't afford the (unbillable) time to do PR for the agency.

When I started in public relations, the seat of your pants was often your road map. What I mean is that PR practitioners tended to place material in a particular newspaper, for example, because they were friendly with someone on that newspaper.

The fantastic growth in public relations should in no way discourage the small company, the new shop owner, or those with a cause who want to fight everyone and everything from city hall to the White House.

Yes, the pie is bigger, but there is still room for the small guy on a limited budget. Creativity and ingenuity still drive public relations.

TALES OF TWO CITIES

The incumbent mayor of Lake Worth, a mid-sized city in the center of Palm Beach County, Florida, was defeated by a kindergarten school teacher/part-time lifeguard in 2005. The victor won with a war chest of a few hundred dollars and seemingly better PR than his opponent, an attorney. However, once in office, the new mayor forgot what public relations was all about, if, in fact, he ever knew in the first place.

In April 2006, a local newspaper published a story highly critical of the city government. The mayor berated the newspaper at a city commission meeting and called publishing the story "irresponsible." The newspaper reported the event and stood by its story. I know all this because I was the reporter of the exclusive story.

Meanwhile, across the country in Scottsdale, Arizona, the scene was just the opposite. The city employs 20 public information officers and communications professionals with a combined payroll of $1.2 million to spread news about the city. In fact, Scottsdale has so many PR people, the city council—at about the same time Lake Worth was being blasted by the media—hired a public affairs manager to oversee all of them. That works out to one public information officer for every 11,750 Scottsdale residents. The large, in-house public relations staff in Scottsdale is needed to disseminate news to an ever-growing and ever-fractured populace, according to a city spokesperson. And it's not just

Scottsdale. The city of Mesa, Arizona, employs 27 public information officers for every 16,666 residents, according to the *East Valley Tribune.*

While Mesa and Scottsdale still get criticized by the local media, in the final analysis, their use of PR keeps them ahead in the public eye.

Following this model, Lake Worth should probably have three or four PR people, which is three or four more than they have.

THE NEED FOR PR LITERACY

Public relations is full of paradoxes. It is a discipline devoted to messages—yet few people outside the industry really understand what it is and how much good it can do. The discipline, which is so good at making clients, products, services, and causes look important, seems to conspire to make itself look unimportant. That may be, to an extent, deliberate. A number of thoughtful public relations professionals worry about the consequences of letting the general public know just how extensively public relations calls the shots.

The most dangerous paradox of all may be that this most pervasive of disciplines is still considered by most managers outside the discipline to be of only passing concern. Managers, business owners, activists, and organizations need to be PR literate and PR competent.

PR's importance is undeniable. When the topic of public relations comes up, the reaction should not be, "We can't afford it," or "What's pubic relations?" The reaction should be, "Now how can I get the job done?"

Public relations literacy is the answer. I'll always bet on the owner of a start-up business who is PR literate over the Harvard School of Business graduate who disregards PR.

It's not hard to imagine that with years of experience in stringing beads, you might get bitten by that entrepreneurial bug to open a bead store to sell beads, beaded jewelry, and to give lessons.

You form a company (aided by a lawyer), lease a store (thank you, real estate agent), work the numbers (a B+ in math), and you're open for beading. But how do you get the word out? In reality, you haven't a clue.

You're thinking the easy (and most expensive) way to get started is by advertising. It's a no-brainer if you have any dollars left after buying loads of inventory and decorating a store. Your local newspaper will gladly design and write an ad for you and charge you plenty. Unless you're buying a full page in a widely read section, you'll probably end up with "peek-a-boo" advertising placement, hoping a reader will spot your grand opening ad.

But if you're literate in PR, you will get more bang for your beads and your proverbial buck by obtaining media coverage. Media coverage gives a business (or person) the credibility of a third-party endorsement to its target audiences.

"Who are we talking to?" This is a perennial question for PR professionals, as it must be for our new bead store owner. The bead store owner shouldn't be talking to those who read the sports section and throw the rest of the paper away.

Today we can segment our target audience as never before to get information on customers, prospects, opinion leaders, and potential bead buyers. This means a lot in shaping a powerful marketing tool.

Public relations was once a shotgun operation. You fired broadsides of press releases, hoping some would get used. That was simple. It was also wasteful. There's no point in hitting folks with your message if they cannot do anything for you.

Today's public relations is different in a fundamental way. Old-style PR was primarily devoted to publicity. To some, publicity was like a four-letter word. "Oh, he's just a publicist or a flack." But publicity was and is a useful and important function. It is also a part of the larger function of modern-day public relations.

These days the main job of public relations may be the shaping of the broader context within which the public in general—or, more likely, specific target publics—forms opinions and makes decisions.

Old-style public relations is reflexive and reactive. The new public relations is innovative. Traditional public relations was always soothing and positive; the new approach is realistic, admits mistakes, and conveys balanced information rather than just puffery. While public relations used to be confined to a limited number of fields, the new techniques are deployed in proxy battles, lawsuits, and campaigns for personal advancement. Doctors, lawyers, financial advisors, and others today use public relations techniques to create images that attract clients. Ambitious men and women are using PR strategies to help shape successful careers.

This book demonstates what is happening, with case histories illustrating the scope, pervasiveness, and power of public relations today. It also shows how to go about it and get big results with small budgets. Above all, though, you will become better acquainted with the giant with whom we had better be friends, if we know what is good for us.

A NEW BREED OF PR PRACTITIONERS

Tenika Morrison of Puyallup, Washington, found herself with a groovy new online vintage clothing store, Catching the Butterfly, but no money to get the word out. That would have turned off most entrepreneurs but not the 25-year-old Morrison. She had no formal training and no funds to hire a PR consultant. Over several weeks she devoured everything she could read about public relations in her local library. "It's been an amazing resource," Morrison says. With the expertise she gained from her reading, she sent out her first press release. It was short and fun, giving the straight details of her new business while still explaining its funky side with a tongue-in-cheek list of the "Top 10 Reasons to Write about Catching the Butterfly." Her efforts paid off. Still she knows her PR work is not over. "I can't just say, 'Hi, my name is Tenika. This is my story, please print it.'"

Sharon Dotson, of Houston, is another of the new breed of PR practitioners. She doesn't belong to the Public Relations Society of America. This former newspaper reporter and magazine editor now works at home and turns out a net income percentage of revenues many times larger than the giants. "I can put clothes in the dryer while talking to a client," she told me. "I have a wireless headset that allows me to move all over the house."

The greatest PR success story of my time, I believe, is the making of the low-budget film *The Blair Witch Project,* produced by two young unknowns from central Florida. With a budget less than it would cost for a college education these days, and handheld cameras, they produced a not-very-good, cheap, hip film that eventually became among the largest money makers in history, raking in more than $250 million. They understood PR well enough to get cover stories in the same week on both *Time* and *Newsweek* magazines in August 1999, among other jackpot publicity. The Internet was relatively new and they knew how to use it to get publicity.

My hope is that you will learn what Tenika Morrison, Sharon Dotson, the *Blair Witch* boys, and others learned. In the rest of this book I will share some tips I learned from working in public relations for more than 20 years, as well another 20 years in journalism.

I will tell you everything you need to know about contemporary public relations so you can do the job yourself, or retain a small, professional firm, all on a modest budget. I'll sprinkle in some tips from some of the big guys too, to back up what I'm saying. And, most important, I'll tell you what reporters and editors don't like about us PR people and why they can't do their jobs without us.

Don't be deterred. The goal of this book is to make you PR savvy. Once you learn the fundamentals of PR you can play the game on a minimum dollar.

Let's begin.

chapter 2

EVERYONE NEEDS PR

"But I Can't Afford It"

"PR is not for us."

"I can't afford PR."

You hear a lot of this every day, from the new specialty food store that recently opened in the shopping center to the small public company whose stock can't get above $1.00 even though the company is making money.

They have their excuses:

- I spent all my money advertising in the Penny Saver.
- All we make are widgets. PR has nothing to do with our business.
- I have no time for PR.

I once argued about public relations for an hour with the chairman of an American Stock Exchange–listed company. They have a great story and spend some $4 million a year on advertising but nothing on public relations. They hired me for six months when their stock was selling for a little over $1 a share and selling about 100,000 shares daily. As a result of some publicity I obtained for them, their stock hit $3 on trading of 1 and 2 million shares a day. The company decided they didn't need PR any longer and the stock eventually fell to under $2 again and trading down to 20,000 to 30,000 shares a day, even while the company was making money.

Small business people and managers need to know what public relations is today and how it works. Not only so they can write press releases, but so they can manage the discipline effectively and make it work with other disciplines to create a more effective, successful organization, small business, or nonprofit group. Had the company with the $4 million advertising budget integrated their marketing program by taking just 1 percent from advertising and placing it into PR, they'd be in a better position today.

Currently, we must foster the spread of PR literacy. Everyone who aspires to business success, no matter how small the business, should be PR literate in today's (and tomorrow's) world. Here is why.

Few executives arrive at or near the top without a decent working knowledge of every important discipline in the company's operation. There was a time when management was considered by some to be totally pure art, uncontaminated by nitty-gritty. Persons who mastered the tools could move seamlessly from one industry to another.

Today, managers need a healthy mix of universal skills and particular knowledge. Self-defense is one reason the aspiring executive needs all-around familiarity, especially as disciplines become more complex. Not that executives are expected to do it all themselves. They depend on experts.

Depend is the key word. It is one thing to depend on your chief information technology officer, research chief, or data processing guru. It is quite another thing to be at that person's mercy. But that is where you are if you do not understand what the expert is talking about. You do not know if you are getting a snow job. You do not know how to apply criteria to performance. You do not know where the money goes.

Managers, small business people, and those running not-for-profit organizations should have a working knowledge of PR. Public relations literacy is important for two reasons: It is growing in stature, and before long just about any organization of any size will have a real PR function, either in-house, through an agency, or with a consultant.

DONALD TRUMP'S PR RECORD

Public relations literacy holds an added bonus. Knowledge of disciplines like data communications and finance are, of course, important to the ambitious executive, but they do not help in self-promotion. Those who know public relations have an advantage in building their own careers, as well as building the strength of their organizations. A manager with PR expertise can use some PR techniques personally and can, in subtle ways, use the organization's PR arm to look better.

Strictly speaking, this may not be altogether kosher. But it is part of the real world. PR-literate executives not only can do it for themselves, they can also detect cases in which other people have done it. And this is no small advantage.

Public relations literacy is spreading. Dozens of public relations courses are taught at the undergraduate and graduate-school level in the United States and in a few other countries. My last book on PR—*Power Public Relations: How to Master the New PR* (2000)—was required reading in marketing classes of a number of universities and colleges.

I wrote in my book, "Donald Trump is this era's most interesting character by far, from a public relations perspective. Trump performed the extraordinary feat of dropping from PR mastery to PR disaster almost overnight."

Trump deliberately and specifically used inflation of his personal image as a business tool. Some headline-grabbing executives rationalize their activities by saying there is a business advantage; Trump actually used public relations as a strategy. One observer said of him, "His image is the strategy."

By becoming famous—and even somewhat notorious—Trump believes he adds value to his holdings. Ordinary people will have some of the glamour rub off on them when they shop at Trump Tower or gamble at one of his casinos.

Trump started doing outrageous things. He jetted around in his own big planes and bought big residences.

Then things started to happen. Some of those were things over which Trump had no control. But even a person totally lacking PR savvy could have seen some of the potential land mines. A respected financial analyst was less than enthusiastic about one of Trump's proposals. Trump called up and demanded that the analyst be fired and, in fact, did get him fired—temporarily. The analyst went public, the company was forced to reinstate him, and Trump looked like a bully and, what was far worse, an ineffectual bully.

The lurid divorce proceedings between the Donald and Ivana Trump—in which both sides rolled up the big guns of high-priced PR consultants—did a great deal in a short time to erode the Trump image. And a series of ludicrous events centering on Marla Maples made Trump look more like a well-dressed sideshow geek than a colossus who had once thought about running for president of the United States. Trump became a figure of ridicule. His superb mastery of public relations had turned to grotesque clumsiness. Then in the late '90s and the turn of the century, Trump started getting his personal and financial lives back in shape.

The Apprentice television show was a brilliant move for Trump. Donald Trump was back on top again. After two successful seasons of high ratings with *The Apprentice,* a number of other business-related promotions grew from the television success.

In 2005, a rumor began that Trump was going to run for governor of New York.

The Donald owes his success to public relations. Before an overflow crowd of more than 4,000 PR professionals and students at the opening of the October 2004 Public Relations Society of America international conference, Trump credited savvy public relations for saving his struggling financial empire in the early 1990s.

Trump's talk underscored the power of public relations to his career.

"Seriously, *Entertainment Tonight* asked me this question. 'Mr. Trump, you're totally brilliant. How brilliant are you?' Now who the hell would put that in an ad, no one would believe it. An ad on *Entertainment Tonight* would cost me like $150,000 for about 22 seconds. If I ever put something like that in an ad, I'd be run out of town," he said.

"I've always felt that public relations is much more important than advertising. You pay $100,000 for a full page and (the readers) don't even look at it. But if they read a story about the genius of Donald Trump, everybody reads every word of it. In one case it cost me nothing; in the other case it costs millions and millions of dollars," Trump says.

INTEGRATED MARKETING

Public relations works best when it is integrated with marketing. In a broad sense, you could say that just about every aspect of public relations relates to marketing. Today there is a more sharply defined category of public relations that involves the use of public relations to support the marketing of goods and services.

Marketing public relations is an idea whose time has come—but the reality is still in the process of arriving. Witness the American Stock Exchange company. This giant spends $4 million on advertising and absolutely nothing on PR. A multitude of companies, particularly small businesses, now acknowledge the power of today's public relations, but they are having trouble applying it.

And a lot of public relations practitioners are finding that their confidence in the discipline is being confirmed—but these practitioners have not yet found ways to adapt their skills to the new situation.

Public relations is a part of the corporate and small business families. But like many recent additions to a family, public relations has had a problem fitting in. There are jealousies and frictions, most commonly between marketing and public relations.

Before discussing integration, let's first try to break out of the mind-set implied by using the labels "marketing" and "public relations." Public relations is a *discipline*. Marketing is a *task*, which is to be accomplished by a number of disciplines in cooperation—sales, sales promotion, merchandising, marketing research, advertising. And public relations.

Public relations is part of the marketing team when it is doing a marketing job. Public relations also does other things that are not directly connected with selling goods or services (although in a sense everything public relations does is more or less connected with selling, as in Donald Trump). Unfortunately, the fact that public relations takes in other assignments besides marketing seems to make public relations a perpetual outsider, the "man without a country" of the company.

The most obvious use of public relations with a product is to publicize it. Stories in the trade press keep the industry informed about developments. Stories on the air and in newspapers and magazines attempt to present the product, service, or cause in a favorable light.

Publicity is particularly important in launching a new product or new business. When you start from zero, the aim is to let the maximum number of potential buyers, users, or donors know what's new in the shortest possible time. Publicity is highly desirable when there are changes in an existing product or service, new applications, services, modifications, or broader markets.

I once worked on the Gillette account, whose Sensor razor launch has been called by many as one of the top ten greatest PR programs of all times. From day one, we sat at the table with Gillette's advertising agency, BBDO, and everyone knew what everyone else was doing. Public relations played a crucial role in the success.

When public relations is used to obtain publicity, it is, in general, supporting the brand, and its messages are created to tie in with advertising and other marketing messages. The media is in the driver's seat in deciding if and when the stories will run. Management doesn't always understand this. They tend to demand that the "placement" of stories be as predictable and planned as the steps in an advertising campaign.

This sort of misunderstanding comes with the territory. Public relations professionals should waste no time wringing their hands over it. The mission is to do the job while gradually reducing the level of misunderstanding.

The larger problem with publicity is that too many organizations settle for it as the be-all and end-all of public relations. Publicity is still the central activity of public relations, but it is not always the most important activity. The discipline can be used in other effective ways to support a brand, service, or cause.

Public relations can go beyond publicity into planned promotion—developing activities, events, and a Web site that bolster brand identification and image. This aspect of public relations is more controllable than the quest for editorial coverage. It can be integrated more smoothly with other marketing activities.

When one thinks of those needing public relations literacy, beginning PR practitioners, small business people, and not-for-profit organizers come to mind. In south Florida and elsewhere, as I see things from traveling and surfing the Internet, I notice a great deal of PR illiteracy in municipalities, hospitals, and other public entities and not-for-profit organizations. It never fails;

whenever I see a successful small city or a hospital, I also see a public relations–savvy person on the scene. On the flip side, those municipalities and hospitals that are often bad-mouthed by citizens and media are minus a PR arm.

PUBLIC RELATIONS AND THE LAW

What about lawyers?

Public relations for lawyers is a relatively new field. When the U.S. Supreme Court ruled in 1997 that lawyers had a constitutional right to advertise, the floodgates for promoting legal services opened across America. At first, lawyers used only advertising to promote their firms. Soon, public relations agencies saw the potential for a new cash cow. Lawyers who had never marketed their services before were ready to pay experts to create media campaigns and newsletters, and to raise their community profile.

Marti Mackenzie, a former executive director of the ACLU of Mississippi, founded one of the first public relations firms in 1988 to work exclusively with lawyers and their clients.

Mackenzie told me she strongly believes that criminal defense lawyers must level the public-opinion playing field against police and prosecutors who have the staff and expertise to convict an accused person in the media before they ever get to trial.

"If a lawyer hires a PR firm to develop a media campaign, woe to the PR person who does not deliver results immediately," Mackenzie said.

Many law firms are now designating a member of the firm to become PR literate so they can get in the do-it-yourself field.

The inexorable growth in the importance of public relations will soon make it a standard subject in any curriculum that prepares people for business careers.

This book is my contribution to that process.

3

BIG AGENCY VS. SMALL
Bigger Is Not Always Better

I have helped manage one of the biggest agencies in the world and one of the world's smallest, and every size in between. Big is not always better (though it's certainly the most expensive).

Often, the only difference between a big agency charging $20,000 a month and a small agency charging $3,000 is $17,000.

I have attended many new business sales presentations with highly skilled colleagues, but after winning the account, we spent very few hours on the new client's business. Some agencies tend to overpromise the everyday services of their top executives. In fact, I left the big-agency world because more and more of my time was spent pitching new business and less on the day-to-day creative side.

Good PR firms are good at presentations. The senior people and the top agency talent spend a lot of time and effort on new business, sometimes giving less attention to existing clients.

The new-business team will have developed a polished dog and pony show. The basics of all effective new-business pitches are pretty much the same: demonstrate a dazzling flair, show extraordinary sensitivity in responding to a potential client's concerns, and promise enduring cooperation and high-level results.

Merilee Kern runs her own small PR/marketing firm in San Diego—Kern Communications—and she loves it that way. "I think that younger and/or smaller shops have less bureaucracy and more flexibility that allows them to quickly adapt with the times . . . new technologies and otherwise," she told me.

Specializing in high technology, Kern believes "technology and the ever-changing Internet space have vastly changed the PR landscape."

"My boutique firm handles clients quite effectively and, more important, successfully all over the country. I've found the client proximity is truly insignificant, and that being in the same city as a client can actually be counterproductive since more time is spent meeting rather than producing. And, again, with the advent of technologies, my small shop is able to provide the same level of service as the giants, but with more flexibility," she says.

Many small firms enter into alliances with other firms in or out of their area and call them in as needed.

Bob Dilenschneider, CEO of the Dilenschneider Group, is an important figure in public relations. The Dilenschneider Group is a partner firm in the Worldcom Group, the world's largest organization of independently owned public relations consultancies, with 91 partner firms and 113 offices on 6 continents.

I asked Dilenschneider for his comments on big agency versus small agency. Here's what he told me:

"The size of the agency makes no difference at all. Nor does the scope, nor the geographic reach of the agency make a difference.

"The difference for any client is really in the people. Do they bring the experience, knowledge, insight, and contacts to a client that will make a difference in that organization's results and bottom line?"

Is big better? I asked.

"Many agencies, both large and small, are stuffed with people who couldn't get jobs elsewhere and whose approach to the field is remedial at best."

Dilenschneider believes clients "should seek original thinking and people who can look around corners and forecast what was coming; individuals who have the integrity to work whatever hours are necessary to get the jobs done; people who can share opinions and come up with better ideas as a result, rather than being polarized in terms of their own views; and individuals of high ethical standards."

Does a big agency benefit because it can put 30 or 40 people into the field to help drive a point of view? I asked.

"Not necessarily," Dilenschneider responded. "It's been proven over and over and over again that one person who understands how to work with the media, outside interest groups, and others of similar ilk can be as effective with six or seven paragraphs and can find ways to protect them over and over again."

Dilenschneider told me a story about the late Roy Battersby who, he said, could work any situation.

"He could send a story to the press on butcher paper with the blood dripping off the sides; or to an editor in Beijing as well as New York on the same grounds as long as he had a story."

Does a big agency help when it comes to generating research?

"Only if the researchers are really good. The small or medium-sized agency can reach out to research sources just as easily as a big agency and often more efficiently," Dilenschneider said.

A Munich, Germany, technology firm learned about me from my last book. The program I developed for them was a big one, too big for my one-man shop. So I brought in a local PR firm to handle some of the details and we were able to put many people on the account.

Patti Giglio, founder and owner of PSG Communications, in the metro Washington, D.C. area, has a small firm but can grow as needed.

"The bottom line is that through strategic alliances, I can offer the same services, only better and cheaper, as the big PR firms," Giglio told me.

"In addition, when you hire me—or most any independent— you get my personal experiences and strategic support engaged in the decision-making process. When one hires an independent PR professional you get personal service from an experienced pro and are never handed over to a junior account manager. I like to say, when you hire me—you get me in a chair. Also, in my opin- ion, it is good to hire independents because independents do a good job or they don't eat."

Veteran PR guru Al Croft of Sedona, Arizona, agrees.

"What's really made it possible for smaller, independent firms to compete with the big ones," Croft told *PR Week,* "is, of course, technology. With the influx of computers and the Internet in the past two decades, it no longer makes a difference where a firm is located."

I can attest to that. When I left the big-agency world and moved to Florida as a lone practitioner, I had more clients from out of state than in Florida.

Sharon Dotson and her Houston-based Bayou City Public Re- lations firm has a similar story. She doesn't go after the compa- nies that earn $10 billion a year; she sets her sights on companies that make $10 million annually. "Winning the trust of small com- panies and getting them to cross the line and do business with me rather than a large, prestigious PR firm is now possible through the miracle of the computer and the Internet," she told me. "By the way, I never bad-mouth any competitor big or small. I only talk about the concept of big firms versus small ones."

The big corporations and government agencies with their mil- lion-dollar-plus PR budgets don't always get it right, according to Linda VandeVrede, who runs her own firm in Scottsdale, Arizona.

"Exxon, Enron, and FEMA had no workable or effective crisis management plan. They ignored the advice they undoubtedly received from their PR staffs and giant agencies. They tried to stonewall with disastrous results."

HOW PR IS BILLED

Big agencies, for the most part, work on an hourly fee basis, like lawyers, after guesstimating how many hours will be put in and what the hourly rate will be of all the people who will work on the account. Every one bills their time, including secretaries.

Here's how one big agency described its budget and fee structure in a proposal to a small, start-up dot-com company:

Two months' fee calculated at $40,000/monthly will be required before work will begin. Based on our initial recommendations and early discussions, we project our professional fees will be in the range of $40,000 monthly. This estimate is based on our combined professional hours. If the client selects programs and activities that exceed this budget, our professional fees will be higher. Expenses are generally approximately 20% of the annualized fee budget. The level of activity and projections for professional fees and expenses will be provided on a monthly basis for approval.

The prospective client had a choice: write a check to the big agency for $80,000 and pray, or go to a smaller, experienced agency at $3,000 a month and pray. The decision is obvious.

When I worked for the Richard Weiner firm—a highly successful national firm operating only out of a New York office—we billed on a monthly fee basis. If at the end of six months or a year we found we were putting in more time for a client than the fee we were charging, we would renegotiate the fee.

At the Weiner agency, if our profits before taxes were 15 to 20 percent of our billings, everyone received bonuses and champagne flowed at the end of the year.

Things changed when the Weiner agency was acquired by the advertising giant BBDO, and merged with Porter Novelli and became part of the newly formed Omnicom group.

Our profits, under Omnicom, had to reach 25 percent. If we were falling short, we had to bring in new business or fire people to make the numbers. Omnicom projected its numbers to Wall Street and all subsidiary companies had to deliver on Omnicom's projections.

Were our clients better served? I didn't think so in the early days of Porter Novelli.

The clients who knew me wanted to see me regularly. However, as a member of the management team, more and more of my time was devoted to bringing in new business and controlling our expenses, and less on creative work.

Incidentally, Philip Morris was one of my long-time clients at Porter Novelli. When we converted to hourly billing, Philip Morris said they had bad results in the past from hourly billing. They told me for them to continue retaining Porter Novelli, the billing would have to remain on a monthly fee basis. I argued to continue billing Philip Morris monthly, and Porter Novelli and Omnicom management agreed. After all, Philip Morris was one of our largest accounts. When I left Porter Novelli, Philip Morris dropped the agency.

Large public relations agencies, like advertising agencies, add people to service accounts and lay off people when accounts are lost. Turnover at the margins may look high, but a prospective client ought to know if there is relative stability among the senior associates and the key creative and research people. If not, why not? Have people resigned, or have they been fired? What happens to the account when a key individual leaves?

Small business owners should note with interest the way the pitching agency talks about turnover. Some will be candid: "He quit because he had a better opportunity at Ruder & Finn." Others will have a battery of alibis—the person who left was just not cutting it. Others may hint at client pressure: "They changed marketing VPs and asked that we shake up the team."

Beware of public relations agencies that seem overly susceptible to client pressure. The savvy client wants an agency that will fight to keep a professional in place, in spite of problems, if they are convinced that the professional is right for the job. "Yes-persons" who promise that the client will have extensive personnel control should not be counted on as strong counselors.

After nodding through the usual litany of clients, the prospect should ask about the ones that got away. Every agency loses clients. How many did it lose in the past year? Who were they? Why did it happen?

These are tough questions. Some PR new-business presenters will try to slide past them by saying there is always flux in the business and that it is complicated to find reasons for partings ways, and often separations have been by mutual agreement, etc., etc. Prospects should not be satisfied with agency representatives who merely parrot the words of the innocuous press releases that were sent out at the time of the change. Agencies should be willing to admit that they are not perfect and talk about their own share in the responsibility for losing accounts.

When some PR practitioners lose an account, they only learn that the client was unreasonable. Good PR practitioners should be willing and able to analyze their shortcomings, draw principles from them, and demonstrate how they have translated these principles into action.

MORE QUESTIONS TO ASK

Clients should also beware of a PR agency that indicates it will continually be uptight, constantly feeling that it is on the verge of losing the account. The agency that runs scared is as bad as the one that ignores client concerns.

Agencies that censor the list of lost accounts have something to hide. Obtain the names of all the accounts lost, and check with the ones that were retained.

PR media expert Jack O'Dwyer says, "Try to compare the current account lists of the agencies with those of several years ago. See how many clients the firm has been able to keep. Rapid turnover in accounts is not necessarily bad these days because of the increase in project work. However, the agency should be able to show a continuing relationship with a good number of clients."

Some firms, when asked what they will do for a prospect, answer with a generality, "Our objective is to make you number one in your industry." But the discussion should go a lot deeper than slogans or broad promises. An agency that has made a real study of the prospective company should have some definite ideas about how its particular strengths can be harnessed to benefit the company.

When asked what it hopes to accomplish, a PR firm should talk about process, not promises. Public relations, by itself, cannot make anyone "number one." But the agency can draw the general outline of a good working relationship.

Here is one way the pitching agency might respond:

> *We want to become your strategic and tactical arm in the areas of influencing the audiences and markets you want to influence. We also want to be able to influence you, to provide you with an input that gives a public relations dimension to the important moves you make.*

Can the $2,000- to $3,000-a-month agency handle your PR needs?

Yes and no.

Obviously, the larger agency has larger expenses such as rent, salaries, and particularly high-priced executives; these expenses are paid for, in part, by the client. The smaller agency may have only a few people on payroll working from a low-rent office, like the sole practitioner, Sharon Dotson, doing laundry while talking to a client with a wireless headset.

The key question, always, is who will be doing the actual work on your account. The big-agency new-business pitch will be made by a star-studded lineup, the top—at least very senior—people in the agency. The makeup of the team that will handle the day-to-day affairs of the client is another matter. When answering the question, "Who will be working on my business?" agencies are often tempted to use certain standard evasions:

- I'll be personally keeping an eye on things (eye-on is not hands-on).
- When you have a question, call and ask for me (to ask is not necessarily to receive).
- Every one of us at the table will be actively involved in your account (until the contract is signed).

Big numbers do not necessarily mean good service. The prospect should concentrate on the one person who will be the captain of the team. One person with brains, common sense, guts, and know-how is better than ten Ivy League drones.

The small agency may be run by someone with vast experience with big agencies where he or she billed time at $250 an hour and now works for half that amount.

Of course, there are plenty of small agency owners out there with public relations business cards who don't know anything about the craft.

Sharon Dotson, like many others, is bothered by poor writing.

"I hate to say it but my experience with young PR graduates tells me that most of them cannot write well," Dotson told me. "And more disturbing, most do not like to write. Writing is the core competency of good PR and that's why I believe a foray through the media world as a newspaper reporter or working for a radio or television station can pay big dividends for someone who is serious about PR."

If you're thinking about retaining a small PR firm, check credentials carefully and get writing samples written especially for you.

The agency should be forthcoming about who will be working on the account and what they will be doing. Again, big numbers do not necessarily mean good service. Will your account person be available on call, 24/7, if something breaks in your organization?

The small agency should be able to talk comfortably about where to get additional staff as needed. Large agencies can point to a lot of bodies and claim they are available on a moment's notice. A savvy, one-person agency, operating out of a cell phone, can obtain freelancers or moonlighters when necessary, and these people can be as good if not better than available staff people in a larger organization.

The agency's professional assigned to the account should practically function as a member of the client company. When Philip Morris was my client, I was given a picture ID card so I could enter their mid-town New York City skyscraper offices at any time of day . . . and I did, many a night and weekend.

If you can't trust your PR person to be part of your company or business, you will waste your money by retaining an agency and then keeping them in the dark.

When a client sizes up the person who will be working on the business, it should be like, in many respects, sizing up a potential recruit for a key job. The person can be a young, bright practitioner or a veteran of many PR wars. Age should not be a dominant factor when judging who will handle the business.

THE EXPERIENCE TRAP

Picking a PR agency primarily because it has experience in a specific industry can be a fatal mistake. This experience can take a number of forms: the agency actually has, or has had, clients in the industry, or the agency produces staff members who can boast of specific experience. Because the idea of a client in the same or similar business may raise questions of conflict of interest, an agency going after a new account may scour the payroll for people who have toiled in the vineyards occupied by the target company. If someone with the requisite experience is found, that person is trotted out as an asset.

Such experience should be discounted substantially, if not ignored entirely. The client company should be far more interested in getting the services of keen, gifted people rather than those who happen to have already been around a particular track. There can be greater benefits in working with a fresh-thinking professional who has a new slant, than working with someone who has well-worn wisdom and knows the industry. Good PR practitioners are quick studies. They can learn the relevant essentials of the business in a remarkably short time.

When pitching for new business, the public relations agency submits a written proposal of substantial length. Such proposals tend to follow a pattern. They state goals and objectives, give a terse recap of strategies, discuss target audiences, and then spend a lot of space on tactics, or the nuts and bolts of implementation. Then, there is a fact sheet about the agency.

Too often the new-business proposal becomes cast in concrete. The people creating the new-business presentation are busy at other jobs, so they save time where they can. One way to save time is by using off-the-shelf material for the bulk of the proposal.

A written proposal that seems truly fresh and innovative, and that is truly aimed at the client without a lot of boilerplate, speaks well for the agency. However, the prospect should not write off an agency just because the proposal seems stale. Many agencies are better than they look in their formal new-business prospectuses.

Written proposals should be more original. Make them shorter, give them visual impact, and shake up the conventional order.

Write something other than the pabulum-prose in similar documents. List a few creative ideas. The company may not buy into any of the ideas but at least it will show some creativity. Or maybe, they'll take your idea without taking you. That's happened to me in the past, but that's the price you have to pay if you want to compete against the big boys.

If you're doing it yourself, or picking an agency, results take time. Don't expect the *New York Times* or *Wall Street Journal* overnight. It can take you or an agency months before seeing results.

If you're the PR practitioner or the client, you shouldn't be satisfied because a big placement is made.

As Jack O'Dwyer says,

> PR firms have a tendency to coast after a "home run"—say a piece in *Fortune* on the first page of the *Wall Street Journal*. There is a tendency for them to say, "That ought to hold them for a month or two." But the client should continue to put pressure on the firm . . . keep feeding them information. Actually, the PR firm should lead the client . . . be ahead of it.

Make the agency give you a monthly report including time spent on a specific task. If you're the PR person, writing a monthly report is a good practice. You should do this even if you are working on a straight-fee basis. The client will learn quickly that an effective public relations program takes a lot of time and energy to reach success. Remember, a PR practitioner's job is to sell to the media, a much harder sell than selling to customers, as advertising agencies do.

JOB HUNTING

If you've just graduated from college and you want to begin your career in public relations, what size agency should you turn to—big or small?

I believe you can learn more in a small agency if you're reporting to someone well experienced in PR. In a small agency, you will be involved in all aspects of the client's business. At a big agency, your day may be spent on one task, such as making telephone pitch calls to the media.

If you work at a big agency, don't let it be a 9 to 5 job. Learn what the other account teams are working on. Take pride in your work. One of my biggest disappointments while at Porter Novelli came after we hit the jackpot for a client with a story in the *New York Times*. I wasn't certain the story was going to run. I lived in Manhattan and shortly before 11 PM, I went to the *Times* building to buy a newspaper as it came off the presses. There was my client's story. I was thrilled. The next day, as the person who worked on the account arrived at work, I asked how she liked the story. Her reply was, "Oh, was it in the *Times*?" How sad, I thought.

After a few years working in a sharp small agency, you can then head for the big time . . . and bigger dollars. Ultimately, you may want to end up back in a small agency if you really love the business.

If you were one of the many who were let go from a daily newspaper in 2005 and 2006, it's a great time to do some PR 101 reading and research the PR firms in your area. They will be happy to see you, if they're smart. With media experience, you should be able to catch on to PR fast and most likely make more money than you did working for a newspaper. And the agency should be happy to have someone on staff with media experience who can write.

One of the key skills to succeed in public relations is writing. Too many PR practitioners today don't know how to write.

The Public Relations Foundation of Texas (PRFT) conducted a survey in 2005 and found that both public relations educators and employers of entry-level public relations graduates were concerned that recent graduates lacked the ability to write well.

According to Jim Haynes, chairman of the PRFT board of trustees, the survey showed that the most visible and troublesome weakness among recent graduates entering the practice of public relations is poor to mediocre writing skills.

4

STRATEGY AND TACTICS
Who Are We Talking To?

If you're a small business person, a big corporation, a non-profit organization, or a PR practitioner, you must answer the question, "Who are we talking to?" This is a perennial question for PR professionals. It is also critical that those learning the discipline of public relations understand the question. You can't just wake up one morning and say you want a story about your company in the *Daily Bugle*.

In this chapter, you will learn about creating objectives, strategy, and tactics, and how to prepare your own battle plan. The tactical tail can never be allowed to wag the strategic dog.

Thomas L. Harris, author and expert in marketing public relations, says, "Once, not all that long ago, strategy was an alien word.

"Public relations plans of the past focused almost exclusively on tactics—the trick was to come up with a Big Idea that would generate headlines."

Today, the word *strategy* is common in public relations. But that does not mean everybody understands what strategy is—and what strategy is not.

Strategy is the articulation of overall objectives along with general guidelines on achieving those objectives. It is where we are going and how we are getting there.

Most people know the difference between the dictionary definitions of *strategy* and *tactics;* tactics are the measures taken to carry out a strategy. In practice—among PR practitioners and in other professions—the words overlap.

Strategy has come to mean a discrete activity that, strictly speaking, should be called a tactic. Sometimes, a public relations professional talks about strategies, meaning news conferences, press releases, and other tactics.

Richard Weiner, PR veteran and author of *Webster's New World Dictionary of Media and Communications,* calls *tactics,* "methods and actions to achieve objectives; different from *strategy,* which is the plan that precedes the execution of tactics."

If this were just a semantic mix-up, it would be of little significance. But it can be more than that. When we think of an event as a strategy—rather than as a way of carrying out a strategy—the event can become an end in itself. This can lead to big trouble and may result in the PR function going off on a tangent instead of sticking to the course set during the strategy-making stage.

DEVELOPING A PR STRATEGY

The basic strategy for a campaign serves as a litmus test for the steps, large and small, that will be taken to carry out the campaign. Every time something is considered—the wording of a release, the appearance of an executive on television, sponsorship of an event—it should be measured against the strategy.

The first question should be: Does this step conform to the strategy? If, for example, the step violates the strategy, then, of course, it must be ruled out instantly. Here is an extreme case. A diet product receives a chance to have "before" pictures of its customers on a TV reality show that makes fun of obese people. This would be publicity for the diet product, but it definitely would not fit in with the diet product's strategy.

When activities are contemplated, they should be judged by asking the question: Is this the best way to carry out the strategy? Or as some say, is this on strategy?

This last question calls for considering alternatives. There are always other ways to deploy resources. The strategy should make people think, at least to some extent, about these other ways. This kind of thinking irks some impetuous souls. They chafe when brilliant ideas are called into question by the question: Is it on strategy? The questioner is denounced as a nitpicker.

Measuring tactics against strategy is not nitpicking. It is a professional practice that gives coherence and purpose to every part of a campaign. To defend against strategy-based objections, the PR practitioner should make the measurement first. No matter how bright the idea looks, if it does not fit the strategy, it should be modified to make it fit. If that does not work, the idea should be shelved.

While developing a public relations strategy, the strategists should ask themselves five key questions:

1. Does it track with the goals and objectives?
2. Can we do it all on schedule?
3. Can we change it if it does not work?
4. Could we do something else that would work better?
5. Can we afford it?

The last question may be the most irritating to creative spirits. Nevertheless, it must be asked—not once, but many times. You can develop a strategy and tactics with no money and then find out you can't afford what you came up with and have to go back to the drawing table. Strategic planning of a public relations campaign should never develop into an ivory tower exercise. Nagging questions must be addressed at every step. Time and money are two constant considerations.

Many planning processes defer the matter of cost until later. The strategists design a great plan on paper. They focus on it, discuss it, fine-tune it, and perfect it. Then somebody says, "Now let's cost this out."

BUDGET PLANNING

Enter the despised bean counters who spoil it for everybody. It turns out that the program, or at least important elements of the program, require more money than has been budgeted, or is likely to be budgeted.

But by now everybody is committed to the program. They have stopped thinking about alternatives. They insist on getting enough money to carry out their plans. Usually, they fall short. Optimistic planners try to achieve results on the cheap. They project what is, in effect, the same program for less money.

When the bargain-priced campaign fails, the PR planners blame the failure on inadequate funding. Not only does the campaign produce poor results, it creates suspicion and bad blood between public relations and other functions, which has a negative effect on future efforts.

The unwelcome—but necessary—art of bean counting should be injected into the strategic process at an early stage. Whenever sentiment begins to coalesce around a certain course of action, the question, "Can we afford it?" must be addressed. And it must be addressed in a realistic fashion, not brushed off or deferred with hopeful assurances that the money will be found someplace.

Budget planning should proceed parallel with program planning. If the budget is inadequate, that fact must be faced. If you can't afford it, you come up with something you can afford. PR people who conduct strategy sessions have to walk a fine line. Good ideas should not be crushed instantly because they are too expensive. Often times, if you address the budget in the early stages, the campaign may develop for less money. If a proposal has possibilities, it should be developed—up to a point. Perhaps it will work in partnership with another company or business.

Building a strategy is a combination of big thinking and practical thinking. Asking practical questions about time and money keep the strategic process on track. These questions combat one of the biggest dangers of the strategy phase—overconfidence. When you are confident and enthusiastic about the plan, you tend to believe almost anything is possible—and to promise that impossible things will be accomplished. Overpromising sours the whole process. An otherwise successful campaign can be deemed a failure because it did not reach unrealistic goals.

Another question that should be asked over and over is: Can we do it all on schedule? It is easy to lose sight of time lines when you are riding the crest of creativity. The strategy looks good. The elements fit together. The total effect is satisfying. Only later, when the strategy has to be executed, do the planners realize that it cannot be done in the time frame allowed. The result is an inefficient scramble.

PR practitioner Linda VandeVrede of Scottsdale, Arizona, tells me, "The positive results of strategic PR are that it enables a company to be more ethical as well as economical because it involves planning and forethought. It reduces the necessity for crisis management or rush jobs, which could involve late fees, rush fees, and legal fees."

IF IT'S NOT WORKING

Strategy works best when it includes measurements that indicate whether the plan is on track, as well as enough flexibility to switch tactics. Flexibility answers the question, "What happens if we find this strategy is not working?"

The built-in measurements should be practical and meaningful. For example, if breadth of coverage is important, then subgoals should be set so that coverage can be measured at points along the way. If coverage starts to lag, then Plan B should be implemented.

All parties should agree on the validity of the strategy beforehand. Otherwise, when one element needs adjusting, the naysayers will proclaim that they never bought the initial premise. Revising tactics is not an admission that there is something wrong with the strategy. Flexibility is a positive attribute. Public relations is often the art of possibilities. When an opportunity opens up, the PR function is ready to go after it—*if* it furthers the strategy.

Public relations people are good with words—sometimes too good for their own good. Some of their best wordsmithing is used to sell the person who is paying the bills, who to them is the most significant public of all.

Many of us are familiar with the public relations professional who is indomitable at meetings. This person dazzles the assemblage with graphics, spins word pictures of magical beauty and promise, and dispels doubts and objections with an easy command of the debater's art. This kind of performance is useful when it is employed to present an idea clearly and forcefully. It is not good when it obscures major problems.

Superb selling techniques can be used—and have been used—to convince organizations to approve the wrong PR strategy. The result? A PR strategy that strikes off on its own, rather than conforming to organizational objectives.

Strategic planning for public relations must start with the stated objectives of the organization. The PR operative who sells a program that diverges from corporate objectives is selling snake oil. As public relations becomes a mature discipline, and as public relations rightfully assumes a more important and respected position, some PR practitioners chafe under this burden. They find it irksome to defer to the company's long-range plans. This means that they cannot use some of their brightest ideas. Some PR practitioners may conclude that the company's strategic thinkers do not know what they are doing, so it is all right to ignore them.

FORMATION OF A STRATEGY

No matter how attractive a PR program looks or how short-sighted corporate policy appears, PR policy must be subordinate to corporate policy. But it does not always happen that way. PR professionals frequently do not know what corporate policy is.

The formation of a public relations strategy properly begins with listening to—not talking to—an audience that might consist of a top corporate executive, the owner of a small retail business, or the key officers of a nonprofit organization, an association, or a government body.

Corporate officials are sometimes to blame for aberrant PR strategies. They are busy men and women; they do not have time to talk to PR practitioners, thus, PR strategists have to learn their ideas about overall corporate policy from various sources—some written, some oral, some out-of-date, some simply erroneous.

When public relations is being used as a marketing tool, there should be a clear-cut marketing strategy available to the PR practitioners. And most of the time, there is. Occasionally, situations arise in which the senior marketing people are, themselves, cloudy about the mission and the strategy. Or they may be very clear on the strategy but unwilling to share it with an outside public relations agency.

I was once retained by the chairman of a public company to create some publicity to distribute to the financial community. I immediately sat down with the director of marketing. She was not pleased to see me and, in fact, would not share her plans with me. I was an outsider to her and she would not acknowledge that I was a member of the team. It made my job harder.

When the larger policy is not clear, it is up to PR to keep at it until it is clear. Sometimes, outside PR professionals find themselves helping to forge policy. A public relations viewpoint can clarify and catalyze the broadscale strategy process.

PR can only develop into the best possible program when it is thoroughly a part of the larger picture. The problem of developing the best possible public relations strategy is particularly acute when an agency has been hired. Typically, agencies make pitches for the business. Agencies that are on the ball make it a point to study the prospect's situation and to tailor the pitch, at least to some degree. Then they make presentations that seem to fit the company's needs.

The agency is hired and the pitch becomes the strategy. This is a waste. The pitch is no doubt very good, but a better strategy can be created after the agency knows the client organization from the inside. Neither the agency nor the client should take it for granted that the ideas put forth in the proposal are the last word. I made many pitches that contained good ideas by myself or with an agency, and, after getting the account, none of the ideas was used. Our best ideas came after we learned more about the client's business. The ideas in our presentation were important because, at least, the prospect knew we were creative.

The newly hired agency should have the guts to say, "We are proud of the proposals we gave you, and we are glad you appreciated them. We want to see if we can do even better. Let us do some fact-finding and then come to you with some new ideas, which we will be prepared to discuss."

The strategy stage, though hard, unglamorous work, is essential and should be carried out with integrity and diligence.

But you say, "I am just a do-it-yourselfer. I have no one to talk to." The foregoing words are aimed at you too. You just have to work harder. Now go back and read the chapter again but this time put yourself in the shoes of both the client and PR practitioner.

Some years ago, I tried to launch an Internet-based Web site selling celebrity merchandise, along with offering celebrity news and information. I called it CelebrityStores.com. Here were my goals, strategies and tactics:

Goals

1. Establish brand recognition for CelebrityStores.com as the premier e-commerce-enabled site that offers a comprehensive selection of celebrity-related merchandise and content.
2. Bolster awareness of CelebrityStores.com among potential investors, celebrity community, alliance partners, future employees, and consumers.
3. Demonstrate CelebrityStores.com superiority and clear ownership in the celebrity merchandising space.

Strategies

1. Determine a unique positioning to differentiate CelebrityStores.com from other companies in the space.
2. Broadcast CelebrityStores.com's strategic alliances with influential industry consultants.
3. Demonstrate technology and thought leadership in the celebrity-related merchandise space.
4. Announce new alliances and partnerships to influential Silicon Alley/Valley media and analyst community.
5. Demonstrate the value of CelebrityStores.com solutions through customer references and case studies.

Tactics

1. Create a CelebrityStores.com news bureau for: key message development, press material development, targeted media lists (business/financial, entertainment, technology, industry-specific vertical trades, consumer), ongoing media relations, awards program, satellite media tour.
2. Develop a speakers bureau.
3. Participate in trade shows and conferences.
4. Look to retain celebrity spokespeople.

CelebrityStores.com almost made it to the starting gate . . . but never heard the command, "They're off." In our early planning we never planned for the possibility of the dot-com bubble bursting. I had it all put together but did not anticipate a dramatically changing economy. The technology bubble did burst, and I went back to my first love, public relations. Incidentally, the concept is just as good today as it was in 1999–2000.

5

BRAINSTORMING

There Are No Bad Ideas

Richard Weiner, a former leader of mine and one of the few to win a Gold Anvil from the Public Relations Society of America, describes brainstorming in his *Webster's New World Dictionary of Media and Communications* as "a technique of generating ideas or creative solutions to a problem, generally in a relaxed atmosphere."

In his new book, *The Skinny about Best Boys, Dollies, Green Rooms, Leads, and Other Media Lingo,* published in 2006, Weiner writes that *brainstorm* was a British medical term for a transient fit of insanity in the 19th century.

"About 1920, the term was used in the United States as a flash of mental activity leading to a bright idea," Weiner wrote. "This evolved into 'brainstorming' as a spontaneous group discussion to generate ideas to solve problems, create names and activities, and pursue other creative purposes."

Over the years I participated in hundreds, probably thousands, of brainstorming sessions with Weiner and others.

Brainstorming is the most effective way to generate many ideas.

I have been brainstorming for years and, to this date, I love it. Besides being one of the most important parts of public relations, it is fun. And it doesn't cost a cent.

The rules for brainstorming are probably the simplest ones in this book.

Brainstorming Rule # 1. There are no bad ideas. At Porter Novelli, the first thing I would say when I put a brainstorming group together is not to ridicule anyone's ideas. Often times, you'll find out the nuttier ideas are the best ideas. Encourage radical ideas. If a young, inexperienced account executive's idea was shot down or laughed at, chances are that person would never open up again at a brainstorming meeting. Think of the story that Mark Twain told about the cat that jumped on a hot stove. "The cat will never jump on a hot stove again. Nor a cold one."

Brainstorming Rule # 2. There are no more rules.

"Brainstorming sessions have the goal of idea generation, which comes from the process of creativity," says Kelly Rice, chief inspiration officer for public relations firm Manning, Selvage & Lee in Westlake, California. "Creativity is a learned skill. It's the power of lateral thinking—using that idea that you had in the shower this morning with something you saw at the playgroup and tying that in to the ad you saw on the subway."

At Porter Novelli, I held several brainstorming sessions every week on behalf of my clients, and I attended many others held by other account groups. I didn't limit the group to account people. I opened every session for secretaries and mail room personnel if I thought they had some creative juices in them. The person running the meeting must be easygoing, nonthreatening, and able to relate to everyone in the group. A brainstorming session starts with a question or problem and ends with a solution or a raw list of ideas.

Most of the time, the winning idea from a session didn't come from one person. Someone would offer an impossible idea, or one that was too costly, but it would trigger someone else to "get a bounce" or "piggyback" from the idea, and change it enough that it was almost workable. Before long, the idea kept bouncing around the table until we had something big for our client.

Think about where we would have been if the original thought had been disregarded? Most of the time, it wasn't one person who came up with an idea, and credit was given to the group.

Brainstorming sessions should be relaxed, informal, and free-wheeling. Laughing is encouraged, but not when ridiculing someone's idea. There is no room for criticism. Fear is the biggest barrier to creative thinking. Groups of five to seven seem to work the best. If you can't put together a group like this, don't give up. You can always brainstorm with your spouse or a friend. Make sure everyone understands what the central question or problem is. A session starts with a clear question and ends with a list of ideas. You can analyze the results later.

Define the problem at the beginning of the meeting. Write down every idea, even the ridiculous ones. A chalkboard works best so everyone can see each idea.

Sometimes you may have to take a break for a few days and allow the ideas to incubate. This gives time for everyone to go over the ideas.

PR wiz Bob Dilenschneider says the basic rules of brainstorming were set down by Bruce Barton of the advertising agency Barton, Durstein & Osborne, better known as BBDO and part of the Omnicom conglomerate.

"Brainstorming is smart," Dilenschneider told me. "It brings together people who are often not kindred spirits and gets them to focus on a problem from their own point of view. But brainstorming is only as good as the person who poses the problem or opportunity. If the problem or opportunity is not put in the proper context, all brainstorming is a complete waste of time."

One of my all-time favorite brainstorming sessions was one we had for General Foods and the powdered beverage Tang with a target audience: Mothers.

We kicked our shoes off and sat around a conference room table staring at a container of Tang. Our mission, of course, was how to revive its fading image and declining sales.

Most people who think PR is just mailing out press releases would simply follow the easy road to failure. A press release announcing the new qualities of Tang wouldn't make it.

Everyone played with the container, as if that would help. It wasn't long before someone suggested we tie in with a cause or charity. Another brainstormer talked about taste testing with the competition. Too risky. Who was our target market? Shoppers? Women?

Finally, we came up with a strategy creating an event specifically directed at the target market. Working with our client and their advertising agency, we made arrangements with Mothers Against Drunk Driving (MADD).

Our big event would be a 4,200-mile march across the country starting in Los Angeles and ending in Washington, D.C., 115 days later. It was no coincidence that the route passed through many of the country's top retail and television markets.

The Tang March Across America for Mother's Against Drunk Driving was a huge success. Daily and Sunday papers across the United States ran stories including some 50 front page stories. Major magazines like *Newsweek* and *Forbes* featured the event. We made local television in every market we touched.

A pair of writers for the *New York Times*—Deidre Carmody and David Dunlop—covered the walk. Their lead read: "What people drink before they get into their automobiles was the issue. What they drink before they leave the breakfast table, however, shared the spotlight at City Hall yesterday." The third and fourth paragraphs of the *Times* article were about Tang.

And Tang, praised by the media and public officials for its concern, got a substantial rejuvenation of its image and a big boost in sales.

Today, Tang is a leader in the global powdered-soft drink market.

Another favorite brainstroming session was the work of a former colleague of mine at the Richard Weiner agency, Jonathan Weisberg. The goal was to come up with an idea to promote the Belgian endive. We bounced around many ideas until Weisberg proclaimed: "Tootsie Salad," inspired by the movie *Tootsie* starring Dustin Hoffman.

A press release was produced announcing the official launch of the Tootsie Salad, which contained Belgian endives (replacing lettuce) and a basic vinaigrette dressing. Weisberg's idea worked beyond anything imaginable. The Associated Press and many food columnists in magazines and newspapers picked up the release, and overnight the popularity of Belgian endives as a salad ingredient increased.

MY SILVER ANVIL

I won a Silver Anvil from the Public Relations Society of America for my work for the Cigar Association of America, an organization of cigar manufacturers. Our cigar brainstorming sessions were even better than the award and more fun than one could hope for.

In one brainstorming session, we dreamed up a book titled *101 Ways to Answer the Request: Would You Please Put Out the #@(%*?!$ Cigar!* The strategy was twofold. First, we wanted to capitalize on the historic link between humor and the cigar. Groucho Marx's cigar was his trademark. George Burns's cigar was his constant companion onstage. W. C. Fields used cigars as an integral part of his unforgettable stage and screen personality. Contemporary comedians like Bill Cosby and David Letterman are well-known cigar smokers. We wanted to show that good guys smoke cigars, and that if you smile at them, they won't mind; they are capable of laughing at themselves. Joking in the face of adversity is an admired act. It conveys good-humored courage and a commonsense approach, which can reduce supposedly calamitous occurrences to their proper size.

Second, we wanted to provide a gentle but definite defense of the cigar smoker's rights. Rather than make the defense confrontational, we determined to defuse the atmosphere by lightheartedness and understanding.

If only there was a snappy comeback. If only you could answer this intrusion with a retort so perfect for the occasion that the cigar itself would taste even better.

The book, I felt, would be effective in itself. If we made it funny enough, people would enjoy it. And the book would also work for us in other ways, such as intriguing the media enough that they would quote it and by providing a rallying point for those wanting to defend smoker's rights.

The ordinary gestation period for such a book might be nine months to a year. I hired a distinguished band of six professional comedy writers, locked them in our conference room, and fed them corned beef and pastrami sandwiches. At the end of one week, we had the text.

An artist provided the illustrations that accompanied the answers to the book's title. The answers were presented in the form of a mock-serious instruction book. The following are some examples:

- The Andy Rooney: "Didja ever notice how the people who ask you to put out the cigar always wait till after you've lit it? Why do they do that? Or after you've put it out? Hey, where ya going'? Wait, didja ever notice . . ."
- The Charles Bronson: "Any other last requests?"
- The White House Spokesman: "We believe it is out."
- The Executive Privilege: "I could do that but it would be wrong."
- To a Lawyer: "I know you're not singling me out. You get paid good money to torment people."
- When in Paris: "Listen, mon vieux, get your fellow countrymen to bathe and then we'll talk."

As you can see, these retorts were not intended for actual use, though I cannot guarantee that cigar smokers have not used them. In any event, the book turned out to be pretty funny. Simon & Schuster published it. The back cover announced, "If Winston Churchill had put out his cigar, we'd all be speaking German today!" The results were gratifying. There was a lot of print publicity. Radio and TV talk shows found the topic sprightly. The bite-sized format of the book lent itself to quotation, enabling us to get a lot of broadcast mileage out of it.

And when people asked about the purpose of the book, we had an opportunity to call attention to the need for more tolerance and understanding between cigar smokers and nonsmokers. We referred people to the rear section of the book, "A Few Gentle Suggestions" to cigar smokers themselves, for ways to be considerate of others while enjoying their smokes.

For years, our brainstorming sessions for the cigar folks paid off. I liked our cigar campaigns. I am proud of what we accomplished on a limited budget for a small industry. We came up with one jackpot idea after another, which resulted in our award. A cigar-smoking boom reversed a 30-year decline in the business and left cigar makers, big and small, richer than they ever dreamed was possible.

HOW TO GET STARTED

"But we have no money," you're crying. "I only have a small bead store. How am I going to brainstorm?"

You can start by inviting one or more of your employees, a supplier, your spouse, or a customer.

The central question should be: "How are we going to get attention in our community and let it know we are here and open for business?"

I'll start it off: How about aligning the business with a local charity and creating some kind of event in the community. Now get a bounce off that.

It may take a couple of hours or a couple of days, but you should come up with a jackpot idea. And you will definitely get better results with the media than if you had simply sent out a press release.

Here's a thought. With presidential campaigns these days starting as soon as the last one ends, it's not too early to start brainstorming for a tie-in idea to tie in with an election. I did this during President Clinton's first campaign. After a brainstorming session, we came up with an idea that was wildly successful, and, I might add, a lot of fun.

My client was an actor named Roger Durrett from Charlotte, North Carolina, who has spent decades performing as Mark Twain. I give Durrett's Mark Twain undisputed second place right behind actor Hal Holbrook's Mark Twain. I first used Durrett as a spokesman in my work for the Cigar Association of America.

When Durrett became a client of mine, we decided after a brainstorming session to run Mark Twain for President of the United States.

With me as his campaign manager, Twain began testing the political waters in New Hampshire late in 1991 in full makeup and costume. Ten Democrats were fighting each other in the New Hampshire primary, a feat that would make the winner the front runner.

Twain/Durrett received more coverage than all the Democratic candidates combined. Front page color photographs proclaimed in headlines, "Mark Twain Considering '92 Run for President as Mugwump Candidate." We garnered excellent television and radio time. We put out a press kit and did all the things that presidential candidates do: speeches, news conferences, walking tours with mayors, flyers, bumper stickers, and *Mark Twain for President* buttons.

During a break in Twain campaigning, Durrett and I went to St. Paul's School in Concord to hear candidate Bill Clinton speak. After his speech, I walked over to the former governor of Arkansas, shook his hand, and said, "My name is Leonard Saffir, and I am campaign manager for Mark Twain."

The soon-to-be president first looked at me as if I was crazy, but after only a few beats, he responded, "Oh, I like Mark Twain. Good luck to you."

I gave Clinton a *Mark Twain for President* press kit. He tucked it under his arm, and I watched him as he exited the school building. He stopped to talk to his aides before entering his limousine and gave one aide all his papers, but I saw that he kept the Mark Twain press kit.

A few days later, I read an AP story reporting on a stump speech by Clinton in another New Hampshire town. Clinton quoted Mark Twain, a quote taken from one of our press releases. And through his two terms as president, he continued to quote Twain, but I will not take credit for that.

One thing that differentiated Twain from other presidential candidates was his fearlessness. For example, Twain/Durrett took part in a display of banned books in Portsmouth, New Hampshire. (And why not? *Huckleberry Finn* was on the banned-book list.)

Another unique part of Twain's campaign was his willingness to puncture sacred cows and take potshots at the absurdities of both parties. Durrett did so always using Mark Twain quotes.

One goal of our Mark Twain campaign strategy was to attract speaking engagements for Durrett/Twain on the lecture circuit. Because of the publicity from the New Hampshire campaign, inquiries flooded in, along with invitations to appear on TV shows in various areas. As a bonus, Durrett agreed to produce and appear in two half-hour specials for the Public Broadcasting System featuring Twain's view on politics. (I helped produce the shows.) Another purpose of the campaign was to say some things that needed to be said about politics and society in America.

I had a third reason, a personal one, for running Mark Twain for president: to serve as a laboratory experiment in applied public relations. The results further validated my feeling that we have entered a world in which people *welcome* the workings of public relations. They are willing to suspend their disbelief to enjoy the sensation of acting, and then are willing to feel as if something is true when they really know it isn't.

The people in New Hampshire and elsewhere on Mark Twain's campaign trail (with, I suppose, a few weird exceptions) knew that Mark Twain was not really up there on the hustings. Nevertheless, they listened as if it were Mark Twain; and they responded to Mark Twain as if he was a real person, expressing their sense of what this country ought to be and can be.

Who knows, with both Democrats and Republicans always vying for their own party's presidential nomination, Mark Twain just may become a third-party candidate again. Put that on your brainstorming table and see where it goes.

6

SPIN OR WIN?

Assume Media Skepticism

While the introduction of a new widget may be the biggest thing that ever happened, a reporter might not care. A reporter should always ask two questions: "Why should I do this story?" and "Why should I do this story now?" If a reporter doesn't ask these questions, his or her editor undoubtedly will. When one handles public relations properly, a reporter's life is made easier. But when one is "spinning," reporters know it and resent it.

Okay, you're running your small PR business and have a client at $3,000 a month. The client says to you, "We have a great message, and the media should be very receptive to it" (or words to that effect). The PR practitioner should dispel illusions about how the world is panting to learn about the company and its products. You may lose a client but it's better than ruining your credibility with the media. You're in business to stay and the life span of your client can be very short. Remember the story about the boy who cried wolf?

We all tend to think the sun rises and sets on our own children. We magnify their virtues, minimize their flaws. It is only natural. Why should parents be objective? But objectivity is healthy in anticipating media reaction to a PR campaign. Editors, writers, reporters, program directors—they are hard-boiled and skeptical. It is built in. They would think of themselves as patsies if they bought a PR-generated story too easily. I know because I toiled in the vineyards of journalism for the other half of my life when I wasn't in public relations.

Sometimes it is hard for public relations professionals to explain this to clients who think of it as an alibi in advance for poor performance. So, PR professionals should not sit around trying to explain it. They should give the client an early understanding of the media. This gives the client a better feel for the real world of public relations. After all, "know your market" is basic in selling, and the media is the initial market in PR work.

I used to tell account executives and junior account executives that they were in the selling business. "Not me," they said. "I'm in PR." Yes, but you are always selling, I told them: to get a client, to keep a client, to sell a story . . . and to keep your job.

It is all right for clients to be enthusiastic about their stories. But clients should not expect PR professionals to share in the euphoria. It is best for PR professionals to operate on a worst-case basis and to make the assumption that there is considerable resistance to overcome. That is a sound approach in both public relations and selling.

Your job is not only to judge the news value of a story but to see how news value can be added to the story. Maybe the new widget isn't news, but someone or something in the company is. "After 50 years in the widget business, John Jones was ready for retirement . . . that is, until a new widget came along." Jones's story might be a nice human interest touch for television or the newspapers. If the widget is plastic, your lead might be something about the plastic industry. If you're selling baby clothing, maybe your lead is about shopping for the hard-to-find gift for a friend.

Consider lining up a local celebrity/politician to purchase the new widget, and get one or two quotes from the celeb.

When writing a release don't forget you are writing a selling piece. Choose every word carefully and then go over it many times. I go over every word. I call it "word-worshiping."

Above all, make sure you don't go out on a limb with a story. Paul Owers, a business reporter for the *Palm Beach Post,* told the following story about a PR firm that issued a news release that began, "With clear skies on the horizon, and plenty of hotels to fill, Florida hotel and resort operators are anxious to see visitors return and enjoy the beaches, Keys and less-than-crowded attractions now that kids are back in school. The problem was, the date on the release was Thursday, the very day that South Floridians woke up to the news that Hurricane Jeanne was headed here." The PR firm thought that after three hurricanes it was safe to tell the story.

Arthur Wilde, the veteran PR practitioner who at one time was a personal publicist for Marilyn Monroe, Marlon Brando, and Milton Berle, once said, "If you tell the truth, even when you conceive a crazy idea, you're better off. If you can't be honest, keep your mouth shut."

THINK VISUAL

Before contacting print or television media, you must think of photo and film/tape possibilities. No newspaper wants to run a firing-line photo of two or three people lined up facing the photographer. You might suggest to the newspaper that a photo possibility might be the owner of the business unloading a truckload of the new widgets. Television coverage of a story needs action. A television crew doesn't want to film or tape talking heads.

Instead of sending out mass press releases—the shotgun approach—think of rifle shooting, one at a time. Reporters and editors like to have an exclusive story. Often times, a story in one medium will get picked up by another medium, and soon you will have what I call the snowball effect.

You can get media attention without spinning. MSNBC anchor Rita Cosby tells PR people:

> Don't be afraid to shoot high if you have a great story. Make the pitch right, and attack it head-on. Keep it crisp, short; and boldface the key points. Make sure it's relevant. Don't bury your lead. Some of these sound pretty basic, but 95 percent of pitches don't have them.

Cosby's biggest gripe is PR pitches that have no place at MSNBC. "You have to pitch on what we cover. So many people send us generic pitches. I'm impressed with pitches that show you're following us."

The *Media Relations Insider,* a publication of the *Bulldog Reporter,* offers the following four tips for killer subject lines that pique reporters' interest when pitching by e-mail:

1. One productive ploy is the use of dramatic flair that invokes an image and piques a reporter's attention—but this approach can backfire if your news doesn't live up to the hype.
2. Another winning ingredient in the subject line is the conspicuous absence of a company or product name.
3. Call out the most distinguishing component—and deliver on it.
4. Demonstrating some familiarity with a reporter's body of work is one of the most potent tools for generating pickup. If you're responding to one of a writer's prior stories, play off the language or reporting used in the piece whenever

you can. You're virtually guaranteed to get your pitch opened.

MERCHANDISE YOUR SUCCESSES

One placement can be a jackpot. When you do get coverage, don't think everyone read the story or watched the segment on television that night. Far from it. That's where merchandising comes in. You will reach more of your targeted audience by reprinting the article and doing a mailing to all the people you want to reach.

PR giant Harold Burson speaks about "PR's love-hate relationship with the media despite the interdependence one has upon the other."

"Press people know they need us to help them do their jobs, a situation that brings about a certain resentment. But let's face it, at times we can be an obstacle, just as at other times we offer valuable assistance," Burson says.

Harris Diamond, chief executive of Weber Shandwick, one of the largest PR firms in the country, sums up spin nicely:

> At the end of the day, PR is about trying to communicate a message on someone's behalf. It is very important that we have transparency in our practices. We have to give very clear guidance on where information is coming from.

PR WINNERS AND POSERS

I started thinking about the best PR campaigns of 2005 when Fraser Seitel, writing in *Jack O'Dwyer's Newsletter,* came up with his PR Hero of the Year.

"This honor," he wrote, "goes to the individual, who during the year, used PR techniques to most effectively communicate a story." His choice: Beth Holloway, whose daughter never returned from her high school class trip to Aruba:

> Single-handedly, Beth Holloway-Twitty has kept the story alive for six months with "fresh leads" announcing her suspicions of the boys brought in, accusing the Aruban authorities of foot dragging, enlisting the governor of Alabama to begin a boycott of Aruba, and so on.

While some criticized her for turning her daughter's disappearance into an "international incident," others said she deserved credit for keeping the story going because, they argue, there are an estimated 58,000 children abducted by non-family members and the publicity gave everyone pause for thought. "Indeed, it's the only hope she has of ever learning what happened to her daughter," Seitel wrote.

Then there's actor Tom Cruise who, fortunately, learned fast from his PR blunders in 2005 and got himself back on the right path. Julia Hood, writing in *PR Week,* reported that Cruise put his sister in the PR job vacated by the legendary Pat Kingsley. "The impact of subsequent PR gaffes was instantaneous, as Cruise became a laughingstock for jumping on sofas on Oprah and taking Brooke Shields to task for postpartum-depression medicating. His romance with Katie Holmes has been called a media plot."

Cruise turned to Rogers & Cowan, a leading film industry PR firm. "He has presumably realized that celebrity PR should be handled by the pros," Hood wrote.

7

THE TARGET
Media and Media Lists

Okay, now you're saying to yourself, "I don't know anyone in the media."

Does it help if you know the editor? Sure. You can possibly get your story through a little faster. Does it help to buy a lunch? Sure. You can always tell your story better eye to eye. But will a cordial relationship with a reporter or editor enable you to get a banal story accepted? It does not. Writers and editors make up their own minds about stories. Editors and writers will talk to those they loathe if they think they can get something good out of it.

Turnover is another factor that minimizes the importance of contacts. Editors and writers move around and get reassigned. Personal contacts are not useful when this happens.

PR professionals once made much of their ability to call editors by their first names. They projected the idea that public relations was done largely over lunch and cocktails, that by buying meals and drinks for media people and buttering them up, it was possible to place almost anything. This is a myth. PR practitioners who try to impress prospects by boasting of contacts are suspect. The goal is to have the brains and skill to come up with story ideas that the media will find irresistible.

PR practitioners talk about placing a story in a newspaper or magazine. The whole idea of placing stories is largely invalid and misleading in public relations. You place advertising because you are paying for it. You try to get editors and broadcast program directors to accept your story. The essence of publicity is that you do not pay for it. Still, I have been known to use the word *placement.*

If you have a good story and your material is interesting to readers in Milwaukee, Oshkosh, or wherever, and if you present it properly, you will be successful.

MAILING LISTS

One of the most important jobs in PR is one that is never recognized or appreciated, whether you're doing it yourself, you work for a small agency, one of the giants, a company, or a nonprofit organization. Preparing snail mail and e-mail lists is a thankless job and is often assigned to the summer intern or to the executive secretary's secretary.

Up-to-date mailing lists are the lifeblood of public relations, yet mistakes that I have seen over the years are commonplace in agencies and companies of all sizes, such as the following:

- Mail addressed to an editor who has been dead for years.
- News releases sent to a newspaper that went out of business years earlier.
- A pitch letter sent to Josie Lambiet at the *South Florida Sun-Sentinel.* (Actually the name is spelled Jose and he long ago left the *Sun-Sentinel* and now works for the *Palm Beach Post.*)
- A letter addressed "Dear Editor" sent to the editor of a small community newspaper by a candidate for sheriff. (The can-

didate had never read the publication.) It would have been simple to locate the name of the editor.

If you have to start from scratch in creating a media list, begin with the phone book and organize your list in categories: daily and weekly newspapers, radio, television, Internet. You can buy—or your library may have—one or more of *Bulldog Reporter*'s pitch books or *Bacon's Publicity Checker*, or other specialized media lists.

My single biggest complaint about PR people is that they pitch blindly—without doing their research.

CHECK THESE OUT

Bulldog Reporter makes life a lot easier. Their 2006 National PR Pitch Book gives you more that 30,000 direct tips from editors, producers, reporters, bookers, and bureau chiefs—most with direct quotes on exactly how they want to work with PR professionals. The listings include direct phone numbers, and fax and e-mail contacts from the lowest beat reporter to the nation's most influential journalists—plus tips on when to call and how to send releases, detailed beat responsibilities, hot angles, pet peeves, pitching preferences, how and when to follow up, and even pronunciation guides for unusual names.

I picked the *Chicago Tribune*, circulation 693,978, at random. Their *Bulldog Reporter* listing is 11 pages long. It tells me that Deputy Editor Peter Kendall covers science and the environment from the Metro Desk, meaning, "I am obligated and want to find a local angle to whatever environmental issue I cover." The listing quotes Kendall, "Pitch by e-mail; if you call, leave clear messages with your number repeated twice."

The *Tribune* listing is in the Consumer and Business edition with sections on newspapers, magazines, regional radio, national radio, regional TV and national and cable TV, syndicated columns, Web sites, and a list of every name in the book.

Bulldog Reporter also publishes media directories on Issues; Policy and Politics; Health, Fitness, and Medicine; Computers and Technology; Food, Hospitality and Travel; and Investment, Banking, and Financial Services.

In all, they publish 15 pounds of listings.

Harold Burson, the founding chairman of Burson-Martseller, says the following about the *Bulldog Reporter:* "We couldn't do without it, because it gives us inside information about what the media are looking for. It saves our people time, it saves them embarrassment, and it helps us place more stories."

UPDATE REGULARLY

When developing your own media lists, radio, television, magazine, and newspaper assignment and feature editors deserve a separate category, as do talk show producers. Another list for calendar editors and a list for public service directors may also prove useful, depending on the kind of programming your organization does. Be prepared to regularly update the names on your list because personnel can change fairly frequently.

Richard Weiner had a lot on his plate every day. That's the price you pay to win a Gold Anvil from the Public Relations Society of America and to be named one of the top 100 people in public relations. Yet he knew the importance of mailing lists. At his agency, Richard Weiner & Associates, and after it was sold and became Porter Novelli, Weiner perused the lists before a big mailing (and corrected an average of 15 percent of the names), and he ordered his mail room to bring back to him personally all undelivered and returned mail. The envelopes went back to the person in charge of creating the lists with a note on them in red from Weiner.

BILLION-DOLLAR PR VICTORY

Grinding out releases for widespread distribution, either through mail or e-mail, is a cop-out. Your company, business, association, or client deserves better than that.

Mass dissemination of news is not a function of public relations. Mass dissemination of news is *the* job of mass media. Mass distribution of releases is a substitute for thinking. Some of the most rigorous thinking in pubic relations is fitting the message to the medium. Editors use stories because the stories are crafted to fit the publication and say something meaningful to the publication's readers. Creating one-size-fits-all releases is the lazy way to do it.

Public relations practitioners who are worth their salt are proud of their ability to match the message to the medium.

I won a multimillion-dollar settlement for a client by getting an article in *Business Week,* not because I knew someone at the magazine but because I studied it cover to cover to find the right reporter to contact.

The case was a lawsuit for $7 billion brought against Metropolitan Life Insurance Company by Patrick Kennedy, a San Antonio, Texas, hotel entrepreneur, for unfair business practices against his five-star LaMansion del Rio hotel.

After two years, his lawsuit was going nowhere and Kennedy and his lawyer decided to use PR because, they agreed, public perception might bring about a settlement.

After I found out that *Business Week*'s number one investigative reporter was Chris Welles, I broached the idea of the story to him. He was interested but cautious. He would not touch it if it was just a dispute between Kennedy and Met Life. I convinced Welles that there were similar cases to my client's around the country. Welles began to check it out, concluded that the story was important, and wrote it—three pages with photos. Included in the same issue was a *Business Week* editorial blasting Met Life.

After the *Business Week* article, the case was covered substantially in the media, including the *Wall Street Journal* and the important hotel and real estate trade press. After that, Metropolitan caved and entered into a multimillion-dollar settlement with Kennedy.

In public relations, we are supposed to precisely define our targets. When a large number of duplicated releases are sent out, there has to be a reason. As a rule, public relations practitioners should be ready to justify every addressee on a list. If the PR professional does not know much about a particular addressee, then he or she should find out whether the publication in question should receive the story.

MORE TIPS

As a service to nonprofit organizations, Chevron Oil offers good media relations tips on its Web site.

Follow-up phone calls are often helpful in placing stories. A good way to start the conversation is to identify yourself immediately, briefly state your reason for calling, and ask if this is a good time to talk. If the reporter says "no," ask when you could call back. Sometimes reporters and editors are relaxed and chatty, but it's still best to have a well-prepared message and to make it as succinct as possible. Even though you sent a release directly to the individual, the reporter may not have seen it and will ask you to resend it. That's a good sign. Or the reporter may suggest you send it to someone else at the newspaper or station. Making a placement on the first try is terrific (and exhilarating). More often, perseverance and many calls will have to be placed before a firm interview is set. On the other hand, if someone is clearly not interested, it's best to take "no" for an answer. If you push too hard, chances are you'll never place anything with that particular reporter, says Chevron.

A personalized letter sent alone or with a press release can point out a specific angle or suggest story ideas or good interview subjects. This shows you've taken the time to consider what might interest that particular reporter. As you work with the media, you will become increasingly aware of the kinds of stories that appeal to various people.

Don't be discouraged if you get minimal or no interest in a given story. It is extremely rare for 100 percent of the media to be interested in a story; and even if they're interested, sometimes reporters aren't available at the right time. Finally, every PR person's recurring nightmare is that a spectacular fire, a hurricane, or a terrorist attack will occur 30 minutes before their good news event is set to begin. If that happens, kiss the cameras goodbye. I know from experience.

It is important to read publications and watch and listen to news broadcasts. Only then will you know if your story is right for the medium. When you read newspapers, look at bylines—who is writing the story. Many writers today put their e-mail address at the end of an article. Take note of those and copy them to your media lists.

KEEP THE STORY GOING

PR veteran Robert Dilenschneider tells me the idea of a list takes second place to understanding how to really develop a story.

It's an axiom in the business that broadcast news follows print journalism. And oftentimes print journalism in big markets such as New York and Washington can be stimulated by a story developed in a smaller market, which is all of a sudden "discovered" in a bigger market. In a like manner, the stories that are driven by publications like the *New York Times* or the *Chicago Tribune*—on their wire services—have huge impact by just reaching one writer. In these cases, a list is completely unnecessary.

Dilenschneider believes the key to any media story is to keep it going over time, making impression after impression, so the audience you're trying to reach eventually understands the story. "In this regard," Dilenschneider says, "media lists can be somewhat helpful. Knowing and understanding the core writers who drive opinion about any given topic is more useful."

Dilenschneider has worked with PR practitioners over the years who insist on knowing everything there is to learn about a reporter. They want to know where the reporter went to college, who the reporter has written about, how many children the reporter has, and so on.

"None of this makes any difference for a reporter of caliber because that individual seeks a story of quality and it doesn't make any difference how well you know or even understand him," he says.

8

ARE YOU READY?

Getting the Word Out

There is no hard-and-fast rule about how to get your message across. The news release is the most effective method, and it is often the most cost effective and easiest tactic of public relations. But, as I have already said, you must ponder deeply whether this is the way to go.

PR practitioner Phil Andrews, CEO of P.A. Public Relations Co., of Flushing, New York City, loves press releases. Andrews told me:

Some years ago I sent an article to a magazine by the name of *Shoptalk.* They featured a story about the Haircut Hut Barbershop Franchise, which I ran for a period of ten years. The cost to me of the three-page story was a typed letter, envelope, and stamp. The magazine space given the article would have cost well over $3,000. Where else can a business get more for their buck in exchange for a little time invested and creativity?

So, if it's this effective, why isn't everyone sending out news releases? The fact of the matter is they are . . . in countless numbers.

The *Bulldog Reporter,* a public relations newsletter, said what a lot of people, this writer included, had been saying privately for years: that PR agencies were turning out a mindless glut of releases, which alienates media sources and demeans the industry's reputation.

The glut is one reason to mistrust broadscale mailings. Another reason is what this practice does to the PR function. Once an editor knows you send out mass mailings, you may never get that editor interested in you or your client again. Huge mailing lists should carry warning labels: "Danger! Multiple mailings can be hazardous to your professional health."

Some of the most vigorous thinking in public relations goes into fitting the message to the medium. Public relations professionals do not get stories placed by taking editors to lunch. Editors use stories because the stories are crafted to fit the publication and say something meaningful to the publication's readers. Writing one-size-fits-all releases is the lazy way to get a story placed.

When a large number of duplicated releases are sent out, there has to be a reason. This strategy should call for the widest possible dissemination, and the story should appeal to the readers of the class of publications on the list. As a rule, PR professionals should be ready to justify every addressee on a list. A mass press mailing is not like a fundraising letter where you hope you will get a 1 percent response. If the PR practitioner does not know much about a particular addressee, the practitioner should find out whether the publication should receive the story.

Sheer activity—particularly the number of mailings sent out—should not be a criterion for evaluating the public relations effort. If anything, mass mailings ought to be cause for suspicion by whoever is paying the bills.

WRITING THE LEAD

Okay, your lists are ready and you're sending out a release. What should it say? First, it shouldn't tell the entire story. No good reporter will publish a news release as is; a good reporter won't even rewrite it. The release should move the reporter to pick up a telephone and call you, or a key person connected to the subject matter, with questions and to get good quotes. So be prepared.

The most important part of the release is the lead, the first words of a news release and, ultimately, the reporter's article. *Webster's New World Dictionary of Media and Communications,* compiled by PR guru Richard Weiner, says: "The most common type of lead is the direct lead, the workhorse of journalism. It may be a traditional, factual exposition, or it may be an anecdote, a quotation, a question, or perhaps a clause, phrase, or single word."

Newspaper editors sometimes write *lede* for *lead.*

A lead should be under 30 words if you want the reader to finish the sentence. Don't tell me the *New York Times* oftentimes runs 50-plus-word leads. They do, and I think they're wrong because it is tough to read articles with long leads.

If you're lucky enough to get a staff writer or editor to read the news release, always remember the lead must be a grabber or the reader will never read the second paragraph.

Vittorio Lanni, chef and proprietor of San Gennaro's, serving family style Italian Cuisine, located at 1201 US Highway 1 in North Palm Beach, announced the new summer menu, beginning June 1, will include 2 pound lobsters for $24.95, and other specialties such as veal milanese and crusted grouper.

Or:

Lobsters are coming to North Palm Beach . . . and they're inexpensive.

Which lead will spark an editor's interest?

HOW TO DISTRIBUTE PRESS RELEASES

Editors like exclusive stories. Instead of a press release, you can send a pitch letter directly to an editor or to the reporter who covers the beat of your interest. Your letter should be as brief as the release and the lead paragraph, again, should be a grabber. End the letter, "I will call you in a few days to see if you are interested in writing something . . ." And, don't forget to call.

"Should I send the release by snail mail (the U.S. Postal Service), e-mail, or fax?" I ask myself this question all the time. There is no correct answer because the media is divided on how they like to receive their mail. There's one big reason not to send e-mail. When you send an e-mail, you have to grab the reader's attention in the brief subject line using only a few words instead of using 30 words in a hardcopy lead. That's a toughie. "Lobsters" by itself may not do it. How about "Lobster News"? I like regular mail unless I know from research the editor or reporter's preferences. Never send e-mail attachments unless requested. Reporters and editors will not open attachments. If you use e-mail, shorter is better.

"No one really reads faxes anymore," said Josh Getlin, New York bureau chief for the *Los Angeles Times*. In November 2005, Getlin and three other journalists participated in a panel sponsored by the Publicity Club of New York, as reported in *O'Dwyer's Public Relations Newsletter*.

"I love getting pitched but I'm not fond of phone calls," said Alexandra Marks, New York reporter for the *Christian Science Monitor*. "We had our fax machine disconnected. We like e-mails."

Lisa Anderson, New York bureau chief for the *Chicago Tribune,* pointed out a problem that many reporters have: "Publicists who pitch the same story to more than one reporter at the same newspaper. This can be confusing and can cause tension."

The group agreed that it's okay to pitch multiple newspapers but let the reporter know that you're talking to other papers.

RELEASE DISTRIBUTION SERVICES

Let's take a look at how a not-for-profit charity handles its PR. Virginia Knor, the director of marketing and public relations for the Western Pennsylvania Division of the Salvation Army, knows firsthand the challenges of generating positive media coverage while working within a tight budget.

Most not-for-profits do not function with large-scale budgets as do many private corporations and for-profit organizations. And most do not employ a dedicated communications professional and therefore are not operating with a sound understanding of the benefits a carefully orchestrated public relations campaign affords. Whether your organization is for-profit or not-for-profit, generating positive media coverage should be high on your priority list. Writing and disseminating press releases and newsworthy items to the appropriate media is the first step and they need to be distributed in a timely fashion; faxes and e-mail attachments do not work.

Knor primarily uses PR Newswire for public relations/media relations to distribute news releases, media alerts, and calendars on a consistent basis. PR Newswire and BusinessWire are two services that distribute the vast majority of releases for corporations and organizations.

According to Knor, in Allegheny County alone, the media coverage that the Salvation Army generated using PR Newswire over one year totaled $6 million in comparable advertising space.

For most PR pros, using a distribution service is almost second nature. *PR Week* reports that distribution services bring in hundreds of millions of dollars in revenue each year and spend millions of dollars on research and development of new products and technologies.

Steven Hacker is building his business by using one of the distribution services. Hacker's company is PassportMD, a portable medical records service that places a subscriber's medical history and files on a business card–size CD-ROM.

According to a column by Jeff Zbar in the *South Florida Sun-Sentinel,* Hacker paid to have the releases he wrote appear on PR Newswire. The cost: $125 a year plus a fee per release, depending on where it is circulated.

As a result, articles about Hacker have been published in dozens of newspapers and national magazines. He was even interviewed by a Japanese reporter, according to Zbar.

Before writing his press releases, Hacker researched how to format his releases and what to include in them. He learned the value of timely story angles. After Hurricanes Katrina and Rita in 2005, when hospitals were flooded and records were destroyed or inaccessible, Hacker realized people could benefit from his product. He sent out a release offering a free PassportMD disc to anyone displaced by the storms.

"I learned what's important: How to format a press release, how to write it, and what to say to get PR tractions," he told Zbar.

The cost of setting up an account and distributing a regional and national release was less than $1,000.

By using one of the distribution services, you most likely will be picked up by one or all of the Internet news sources such as Google, Yahoo, or AOL. Remember, their visitor numbers far exceed the circulation of most newspapers.

When writing a release for a distribution service, use key words that a search engine will pick up. If you use a competitor's name because it is better known than yours, it may help get your story picked up.

THE KEY TO THE PR EDGE

Fraser Seitel has been a communication consultant, author, and teacher for more than 30 years. He offered some thoughts about news releases, as well as his taboo list, in a column for *Jack O'Dwyer's Newsletter.* Seitel says:

> It is quite true, despite journalistic denials, that the media would have difficulty functioning without press releases. The vast majority of the content in any daily newspaper—upwards of 80 percent—originates in the form of a press release from a company, politician, agency, association, or individual.
>
> But just because reporters depend on press releases doesn't mean they have to like them. And they don't. In fact, by and large, reporters hate press releases—often for good reason.

Seitel says "most releases are thrown together with little forethought for niceties like grammar and punctuation and spelling."

The following "patently offensive" terms should be considered taboo in all but the most unusual circumstances, according to Seitel:

- *Leading.* Everyone considers themselves "leading." So drop it.
- *Going forward.* Can you ever go any other direction?
- *Unique.* C'mon, that ain't unique.
- *Breakthrough.* Like unique, it must be a demonstrable breakthrough.
- *Revolutionary.* That's too much of a stretch.

- *Cutting edge.* This one has really gotten out of hand.
- *State-of-the-art.* See *Cutting edge.*

One of the challenges for PR practitioners these days is getting reporters to open their e-mails. The vast majority of e-mails sent to the media never get read. If PR practitioners' e-mails don't get read, there is no shot at getting the publicity they so desperately need.

Bill Stoller of the Publicity Insider has come up with what he calls, "The ultimate PR Edge to get that precious coverage."

According to Stoller, the key to getting your e-mail opened and read is the subject line. "No matter how on-the-money your pitch, a sub par subject line will kill any chance of getting the reporter's attention You've got one shot at getting your e-mail opened; make the most of it with a killer subject line," Stoller says. He offers the following three tips:

1. Place the word "News" or "Press Info" or "Story Idea" at the beginning of your e-mail subject line.
2. Try to incorporate the reporter's first name at the beginning of the subject line.
3. If you know the name of the reporter's column, for instance, "Cooking with Linda," try to incorporate it into the subject line.

And when you write food editors, leave out adjectives like "most delicious" and "heavenly tasting"; reporters don't like being sold with overly promotional language. Do try to use information about the product or company in the context of industry trends. Reporters prefer to write about trends rather than products.

Make the information you place in the subject line short and to the point. Often, reporters' e-mail software cuts off the subject at only a few words. Don't be cute or vague in your subject line.

For example, "Here's a Great Story!" is vague and sounds like spam; "This will win you a Pulitzer!" will make you look silly.

Don't include more than a short pitch letter or press release in the body of your e-mail; watch for typos or grammatical errors; don't include an attachment with your e-mail. In this day and age of sinister viruses, reporters automatically delete e-mail with attachments, says Stoller. Don't place the following words by themselves in the subject line: "Hi" or "Hello"—the media's spam filters will pounce and destroy. And don't send an e-mail with a blank subject line. Do include all your contact information.

IT'S OR ITS?

Most journalists use the *Associated Press Stylebook*. I'm sure you know the AP, the organization about which Mark Twain once wrote: "There are only two forces that can carry light to all the corners of the globe—only two: The sun in the heavens and the Associated Press down here." The AP's stylebook is a small investment that will improve your press release writing. The book contains more than 3,000 A-to-Z entries and includes the AP's rules on grammar, spelling, punctuation, capitalization, abbreviation, and word and numeral usage. The book is regularly updated to include new entries like 9-11, ground zero, and SAR.

Norm Goldstein, a veteran AP editor who oversees the stylebook, talked to the Public Relations Society of America's "Tactics" publication about e-mail and whether PR practitioners are getting better at communicating, perhaps becoming even better writers.

It's probably just the opposite. Because of the increased communication we're getting more careless. It's so easy to do and it's so quick to do that you don't take the time to develop a thought or worry about how you're writing it. And there are built-in errors. Even when you deal with spell check in your e-mails, or anything electronic, you've lost a lot because you're giving away the responsibility for your writing to an electronic system. It doesn't catch all punctuation. Because of the benefit of computer writing and Internet writing—the speed—we get careless about it.

What's the most common mistake in writing?

Goldstein says the one that bothers him the most—because it appears to be the simplest to understand—is punctuation of the word "its." I-T-apostrophe-S or I-T-S without the apostrophe. "It's gets so universally confused. Spell check won't catch it. It's probably the most common error I see," Goldstein said.

THE SEARCH ENGINE: A MUST

If you're not using Google regularly, start now. This fabulous search engine will make your life easier and everything it does for you is free. "Google is now processing roughly one billion searches per day," writes Tom Friedman, the Pulitzer Prize–winning author and *New York Times* columnist, in his best-selling book, *The World Is Flat.* Friedman quotes Alan Cohen, a wireless technology executive:

"If I can operate Google, I can find anything. Google is like God. God is wireless, God is everywhere. And God sees everything. Any question in the world, you ask Google." I couldn't agree with anyone more than Alan Cohen, as quoted by Friedman.

Try searching Google for recent stories that have appeared relating to the industry or field of your interest. If you're too busy to search Google on a regular basis, it will help you out (still for free) through Google Alerts. Tell Google your key words—as many as you want—and it will e-mail you alerts every day on new postings of the topics of your interest.

Other search engines—Yahoo, Microsoft, and ask.com—are good too. And try this one, *www.dogpile.com.* It is all the best search engines piled into one.

DOS AND DON'TS

Actually, this entire book is made up of dos and don'ts. If I'm repetitious in this chapter and book, it's by design. Read it over and over again and you, too, will master today's PR. To err once, is how I learned; to err twice, shame on you and me. Here are some dos and don'ts:

- Do read everything, in print and online, that you can, particularly publications related directly to your work.
- Don't make promises to the media and clients you can't keep.
- Do distribute news that is relevant.
- Don't make inflated claims.
- Do tailor your pitch to the media.
- Don't make vague statements.
- Do remember the media loves a good story.
- Don't talk down to the media.
- Do make certain you have correct addresses and spelling of names.
- Don't avoid a reporter's phone call if you're afraid of the call's subject matter.
- Do keep your pitches short and to the point.
- Don't send attachments with your e-mail.
- Do use quotable quotes.
- Don't complain if the reporter gets something wrong (unless a retraction is warranted, and then be very diplomatic).
- Do include contact details for further information.
- Don't pester an editor to use a press release.

- Do use a headline or subject line that quickly conveys what the press release is about.
- Don't pad a press release or pitch letter with unnecessary copy.
- Do use the method of delivery (snail mail, e-mail, fax, Fed Ex, etc.) that your media contact prefers. If you don't know, find out.
- Don't use ALL CAPS in your press release.
- Do proofread all e-mail and press releases.
- Don't call a reporter/editor and ask if the publication used your press release.
- Do double space all press releases.

LETTERS TO THE EDITOR

PR News published some excellent tips for writing letters to editors, as developed by Anne Klein and Associates, such as the following:

- Keep it short: Because these letters are so popular, editors receive an abundance of them. Keeping it to a 250-word maximum helps get it printed.
- Keep it factual and rational: Because a letter to the editor expresses your view on an issue, you want people to find it credible. Support your opinion with facts that will help convey your message.
- Catch and keep the audience: Start with a strong assertive message to hook the reader.
- Identify yourself: Most publications require letters to have a name and address.
- Respond quickly: Whether writing to respond to an article or to voice your opinion on a current topic, get it in the hands of the editor quickly. Check to see if the editor accepts fax or e-mail.

When I worked for Senator Jim Buckley, I accompanied him on a trip to the Soviet Union during the cold war. I was warned that our hotel room would be bugged. I was told that, if we wanted to communicate confidentially, we should bring along two children's writing slates, the kind where the writing disappears the moment the plastic sheet is raised. I wrote a letter to the editor of the *New York Times* of our experience. It was a fun story that I thought the *Times* would appreciate. The letter was published with a headline, "How Porky and Bugs Outwitted the Russians."

If your interest is more than the local media, you should familiarize yourself with the national print and broadcast media.

Here is a circulation ranking of the top 20 major U.S. dailies in 2005:

1. *USA Today* 2,296,335
2. *Wall Street Journal* 2,083,660
3. *New York Times* 1,126,190
4. *Los Angeles Times* 843,432
5. *Daily News,* New York 688,584
6. *Washington Post* 678,779
7. *New York Post* 662,681
8. *Chicago Tribune* 586,122
9. *Houston Chronicle* 521,419
10. *Boston Globe* 414,225
11. *Arizona Republic* 411,043
12. *San Francisco Chronicle* 400,906
13. *Star-Ledger,* Newark, New Jersey 400,092
14. *Star Tribune,* Minneapolis-St. Paul, Minnesota 374,528
15. *Atlanta Journal-Constitution* 362,426
16. *Philadelphia Inquirer* 357,679
17. *Detroit Free-Press* 341,248
18. *Cleveland Plain-Dealer* 339,055
19. *Oregonian,* Portland, Oregon 333,515
20. *San Diego Union-Tribune* 314,279

E-mail me the good news when you get ink in one of the above (*Lenpr@bellsouth.net*).

SPECIAL EVENTS

In your brainstorming session, you should address the possibility of using a special event to get the word out. I agree with the way public relations consultant Craig Miyamoto, of Honolulu, describes special events:

> Special events have always been . . . well, special to me. Ever since taking a "Water Week" bus tour on my first day as deputy public relations director of the Honolulu Board of Water Supply, I have found no other public relations tactic/initiative that captures your imagination, stirs up your blood, gets more people involved, excites the public, causes you more headaches, drains your energy, brings tears to your eyes, makes blisters bloom, and just plain satisfies more, than special events.
>
> The genre is unique. Part of what you do is a holdover from great events of history, from Biblical times to the American Revolution, from the days of P.T. Barnum's press agentry to Woodstock II—full of showmanship and hype, while serving as a serious and effective means of communication.

Whether you're planning a booth at a food exhibition, a 10K walk, an annual dinner for your stockholders, a college career day, a county fair, a groundbreaking ceremony, a conference, a Farm Aid concert, a MADD March Across America, a National Save Your Vision Week, a centennial celebration, a Better Sleep Month, an exhibit of Egyptian artifacts, or an academic symposium, you are faced with the challenge of pulling together a talented mélange of suppliers, freelancers, company employees, and temps into a team that operates like the delicate innards of a fine Swiss watch.

So where do you begin? Begin at the beginning. Break the project down into manageable parts.

The four steps in the public relations process are research, planning, communication tactics, and evaluation. It's the magic formula. You can use it for whatever project or activity you're dealt in life. However, let's make a few changes: The four steps in the *special events* process are research, planning, event execution, and evaluation. It's what will get you through this monstrous undertaking. So go ahead. Get to work.

VIDEO NEWS RELEASES

Video news releases, or VNRs as they are often called, are video clips that are indistinguishable from traditional news clips. VNRs are sometimes screened unedited by television stations without the identification of the original producers or sponsors who are commonly corporations, government agencies, or nongovernmental organizations.

The VNR is a carefully constructed 90-second to 2-minute videotape that meets television standards for usability. It projects the message of the VNR's producer within the framework of a standard TV news story. The VNR promotes your product, service, or cause, or tells your story in a way that makes it seem like a legitimate news item, not a plug.

VNRs are widely used in newsrooms. VNRs are produced like a regular news story and relay a product launch, medical discovery, corporate merger event, timely feature, or breaking news directly to television news decision makers who may use the video and audio material in full or edited form. Most major television stations now use VNRs, some on a regular basis according to Media Link, one of the major VNR producers. While expensive compared to the cost of traditional news releases, they allow sponsors to present their message without it being filtered by journalists. VNRs are commonly used unedited by small regional television stations that have limited budgets for news production or are understaffed. While some stations have a policy of not using VNRs, public relations practitioners commonly cater to this by also providing a series of clips designed to be used as stock footage.

Larry Moscowitz, the founder of Medialink, candidly said the use of VNRs was widespread.

> We determined prima facie and scientifically and electronically that every television station in America with a newscast has used and probably uses regularly this material from corporations and organizations that we provide as VNRs or B-Roll or other terminology we may use.

Even the White House creates VNRs. Following a March 2005 *New York Times* report on governmental use of VNRs, White House spokesman Scott McLellan was asked at a media briefing whether VNR use was "legal and legitimate" . . . without disclaimers that they're government productions, as long as they meet some standard of factual basis. He responded:

> First of all, we're talking about informational news releases, and the Department of Justice has issued an opinion saying that as long as this is factual information about department or agency programs, it is perfectly appropriate.
>
> And my understanding is that when these informational releases are sent out, that it's very clear to the TV stations where they are coming from. So that information, as I understand it, is disclosed. And the Justice Department opinion talks about the importance of making sure that it is factual information and not crossing the line into advocacy.

Video news releases are not cheap. Here are some of the questions to ask before investing in a VNR:

- Does the topic have a news angle? Is it about a technological breakthrough? Does it make life easier? Does it demonstrate an emerging trend? Is there something humorous or touching about the topic?
- Can the story be told in two minutes or less? Does it have interesting visual elements?
- Is the topic sufficiently different enough to appeal to a producer?
- Will exposure on TV news shows help sell the product, service, or cause?
- What sales promotions can be tied in with the exposure?
- Is the VNR important enough to warrant the cost ($20,000 to $40,000 or higher)?

VNRs should be produced by independent video producers who have worked in TV news. The VNR is not for inexperienced people. Making good VNRs is a specialized art that fits promotional needs with broadcast news ground rules. The producer has to have the experience and feel to put in enough objectivity to induce a television show to run the piece.

You want to get the VNR to TV stations in all the areas where you want the message to air. If your list is not very big, you should rethink the expense of the VNR and consider simply trying to pitch your story to a TV news producer.

You also might consider sharing the costs of a VNR with another company or cause, if it is an appropriate fit.

Satellite Media Tours (SMTs) are another way to cover a large area. They are a series of prebooked, live, one-on-one interviews that place your spokesperson on television from the comfort and convenience of one location. Your story can achieve unparalleled broadcast audience exposure in only a few hours at a reasonable price. Media Link is also a major provider of SMTs.

TARGET AUDIENCES

According to PR veteran Bob Dilenschneider, the main goal is reaching a finite audience that can have a real impact on the problem or opportunity: "That's what communications is all about."

Dilenschneider believes that, generally, the audience for most messages, unless the message is a part of a consumer marketing program, is less than 10,000. "Understanding who those people are and how to reach them is the key," he says.

He says his firm has run programs for less than $25,000 that have had a global impact, and his firm has run programs for over a half million dollars that have to stretch to be heard.

According to Dilenschneider, "If someone knows what they're doing and applies resources in a proper way against just a few 'gatekeepers' who help mold public opinion, they can get the job done on a budget."

9

THERE'S MORE OUT THERE THAN THE *NEW YORK TIMES*

Television, Radio, Community Newspapers, and Newsletters

Too many public relations practitioners forget television, radio, and the weekly newspapers. Television and radio are penetration media. Television slices through the clutter to affect the viewer (and radio, to an extent, slices through the clutter to affect the listener). Even if your business or organization is small, you can build sales and awareness by having your product or service discussed on the air in a nonadvertising context.

TELEVISION: WHAT WOULD WE DO WITHOUT IT?

By and large, television is the best place to be. By using tested approaches (and avoiding certain pitfalls), you can make the reach and power of television work for you.

Television is always looking for interesting settings and interesting people who have something interesting to say, and who say it well. The great proliferation of 24-hour news shows and talk shows gives companies and all kinds of organizations a chance to project an image and tell a story on the most effective media. Thousands of guests are booked on to American radio stations every day as guests on all kinds of shows.

Television requires that the sell not be too blatant, that the performer be entertaining and instructive, and that the information and opinion presented by the performer be valid.

I use the word *performer* advisedly. The performer on a TV talk or news show is there to help the show attract an audience and sell advertising. The performer may be CEO of a super powerful, multinational corporation, but if the performer is long-winded, boring, or unhelpful, television is not interested. On the other hand, if the performer has a great personal story to tell about a life that was saved by using seat belts, the program director will be interested.

Unlike print media, TV talk shows and news programs have a symbiotic relationship with PR practitioners. Television is willing to allow itself to be used to promote products, new businesses, books, movies—whatever. Put an author on the *Oprah Winfrey Show* and the book becomes an automatic best seller.

Newspaper people, on the other hand, say, "I'm not your partner." They're always afraid that by writing a story about your new business, they will help raise money for you or get your business off the ground.

If you want TV exposure to promote a particular product, look for the things about the product that might be interesting or amusing to the TV audience. What is new and different about it? Does it tie in with some current trend? What differences can it make in people's lives? How was the product or service developed? What need is being met? Can you think of any interesting anecdotes about the product, its users, or those who produce it?

Maybe you are not promoting a particular product but, rather, a whole company. What is interesting about the company to the casual TV viewer? This question must be answered objectively. The people involved with the business or nonprofit think that every little detail is of interest. Alas, the world at large couldn't care less about the nuts and bolts of an organization.

Maybe the company, through its TV representative, can provide something of real use to the audience—something above and beyond the utility of what the company sells. A manufacturer might have helpful things to say about how to use and care for household tools and appliances. A bank might offer tips on security. A company in the food industry could provide information on nutrition, diet, and preservation. The key to media-worthiness is objective information that entertains and helps the audience.

Keep up-to-date on current events. You might be able to add a local or expert angle to a breaking story.

THE TELEVISION SPOKESPERSON

A spokesperson must be someone with authority and credibility—the chairman, the president, a senior executive, the owner. If the subject is special or technical, the spokesperson should be the company's leading expert.

The spokesperson should be attractive and articulate. Visual impact is more than 80 percent of television's effect. A person who speaks well but looks shifty or insignificant will not make a good impression. It is better to pick someone who looks good. People can be taught to talk effectively on television.

Brevity is essential. The standard format is Q&A. The TV host, reporter, or anchorperson asks a question. The guest should answer with a short, punchy statement, 30 seconds or less, and then add detail only when appropriate. Long, detailed explanations do not work well on television.

Mobility is also essential. When nonprofessionals appear on television, they tend to become rigid. Only their lips move. Television is a visual medium; it requires movement. Television spokespersons should move around in their chairs (although the head should always be absolutely vertical, not on a slant). They should smile and nod their heads. They should move their hands, lean forward, and listen carefully.

Coolness is another requirement. The spokesperson is there to put on a show and project a desired impression. The TV host asking the questions will not be familiar with—or interested in— the particular details of the message. Typically, the host comes into the studio 30 to 60 seconds before going on the air, glances at the press release or backgrounder, and starts asking questions. The guest should be ready with punch responses (not jokes), anecdotes (the more anecdotes, especially about people, the better), and plausible answers to all the questions that might reasonably be asked.

It is all right for the spokesperson to mention the company and its products, as long as the mentions are not too forced and not too frequent. I once put together an event for my client Philip Morris at the Vietnam Wall in Washington, D.C. I hired Bob Hope (for $60,000) for the outdoor ceremony in front of hundreds of Vietnam War vets. Before Hope spoke, Philip Morris's president delivered some remarks. He mentioned the name Philip Morris more times than he should have. Ted Koppel, the ABC TV newscaster, was the master of ceremonies. After the event, Koppel told me and Linda Wallen, my supervisor on the account, "I was going to kick your president in the shins if he mentioned Philip Morris one more time."

Visual demonstrations are better than mentions. Show the product in operation. Show photos or film. Show graphs and charts . . . but treat them gently. I was campaign manager once for New York State Senator John Marchi who was running for mayor of New York City. For a television appearance, we prepared a large chart on growing crime in the city. Marchi is a soft-spoken person and I knew I had to get him charged up if he was to be effective. I told Marchi to express a little anger when he was using the chart. He got carried away. His hands started flailing and he knocked the chart off the easel. I was standing with his daughter in the back of the room, and she thought her father was going to have a heart attack.

The spokesperson is the embodiment of your business or organization on the air. That person should project innovation, reliability, and integrity. For local promotions, it is usually best to use someone from your own organization—someone who does well on television and radio and can speak authoritatively about the subject matter. For national promotions, it is probably best to select a "name"—someone who is a known quantity to program directors.

Public relations spokespersons must have experience, if not expertise, with the products or services they are promoting. Here, public relations differs sharply from advertising. At Porter Novelli, we used former New York Yankee Mickey Mantle as a spokesperson for the U.S. launch of an arthritis drug. He told a *Today* television show audience that the drug helped him play golf again. He also said it helped him cure a hangover. This ad-lib was not greeted with enthusiasm by the competitors.

Requesting to be on a local TV station should be done in writing. Do not call up the program director and say, "Hey, you ought to have us on your news show." Local TV executives are very good at turning down such advances in the nicest possible way. (Newspaper editors are not as nice.)

Prepare a press kit. The kit should contain, at a minimum, a pitch letter; the biography of the spokesperson; a 5" × 7" glossy black-and-white or color photo with caption; a release or backgrounder; and a fact sheet. If there's too much in the kit, however, the material might not get read at all.

RADIO

Radio interviews can reach a specific audience with in-depth motivational messages. Most of the all-news and all-talk stations are on AM. If you are trying to reach a businessperson audience, morning (7 to 9:30 AM) and evening (4 to 7 PM) drive times are primary targets. If your target audience consists of people likely to be home during the day, you may find it easier to arrange an interview, because more PR practitioners are vying for drive time. If your message is compatible with the station's profile, go for it. Otherwise, concentrate on the network-affiliated and independent stations with the biggest wattage and the highest listenership.

Late-night radio has become a good place for placing spokespersons for interviews. Listen to the show! Be sure your spokesperson and message will be treated courteously. Make sure that you are comfortable with the atmosphere of the show.

Some PR practitioners send releases to all radio and TV stations. This is a waste of time and money, and it erodes credibility with the stations. Radio and television stations are as diverse as sections in a newspaper.

Build compartmentalized lists of broadcast outlets, or keep your list culled to those stations whose formats suit you. There are thousands of radio stations. Your likely market is news/talk or all-news stations. Focus on them. Tailor your pitch letter to the particular radio station. Keep it short. It should be no more than one page.

When you advertise, you have a guarantee that your commercials will run. There are no guarantees in public relations. However, your chances will increase if you pitch for time that the stations find difficult to fill. Saturdays and Sundays are slowest for broadcast. July and August are the easiest times of the year to place spokespersons; stations are scrambling for guests during these months because that's when the audience is smallest.

A 30-second guest spot on a talk radio program could put your boss, source, or expert in front of millions of Americans because some 20 million people listen to radio each week—and talk radio listeners tune in about 21 percent more than other listeners. Take, for example, *CNN Radio*'s extensive reach: "We have 2,000 affiliates nationwide—spanning everything from little sports stations on the AM dial to big FM stations in Los Angeles and New York," shares senior producer Sherri Maksin.

In an interview with *Bulldog Reporter,* Maskin explained how to tap into that huge audience. She offered the following quick list of traits she says prospective guests must have to make the cut in radio. Read on to make sure your source has what it takes:

1. Great guests are available 24/7. Print journalists regularly complain that sources and even PR practitioners aren't available when they call. It's the same in radio—but amplified: If you're [pitching] a client, he has to be available at any hour of the day . . . or night. This will give him a higher chance of getting on the air.

2. Great guests have been vetted by other media. When I'm looking for a guest, I'll just cold call people. I'll read the newspapers every day and just call them cold and interview them. I do that every day—read the papers [and look for sources]. For example: I'm going to do a special in two weeks on the bird flu and every day I've been reading about it in the newspapers. I look at the articles where people are quoted. I write those people down, their names—and then I try to find them. Similarly: In the pitch, be sure to say, "[My expert] also appeared on this or that show." I like that—knowing what other shows guests have appeared on.

3. Great guests put their credibility online. One way to push sources to the top of the media's "consider" pile is to help producers find them. For example, post your prospect's clips online.

4. Great guests are conversational. I always do a pre-interview because a guest might "sound" great in print. But then when you hear him, he doesn't sound too good. Or a [prospective guest] might have a really thick accent. That just doesn't translate to radio. Even though a source is an expert and is great in what [is being said]—it's not going to work if he has a thick accent. Guests have to be able to have easy conversations. They have to know how to speak [clearly] and speak in concise, short sentences. We watch for people whose conversations are dragging. We need to know that before we go on the air or we could wind up in disaster. These pre-interviews are so important, because we're looking at how a [person] holds a conversation.

5. Great guests tie to the day's news. Right after everything happened in New Orleans following Hurricane Katrina, a few PR companies called me with experts on things like how to fix the levee. One person in particular offered to talk about the whole race thing that happened. It was so specific. It was exactly what I wanted—and it was a great pitch. They e-mailed me and [it was relevant to] the news of the day. At the same time all of the New Orleans stuff was happening, a PR guy called me and pitched [someone to talk about] phone accessories. I'm like, here is Katrina and that [idea] is ridiculous. I just said, do you know what's going on in the news? I hung up on him. Just don't do that. Watch the news and know what's going on.

PHOTO SHOOTS

Yes, a picture is worth a thousand words. You may not have a story but you can offer an editor a great photo opportunity. A friend of mine became the Jacuzzi hot tub distributor in Palm Beach County, Florida. He asked me how he could get a few words on the business page. I told him that Jacuzzi's would not be very exciting to the two daily newspapers in the county. I suggested inviting some models from a local agency or actresses from a community theater group or runners prepping for the Palm Beach Marathon to his Jacuzzi showroom for a relaxing hot tub dip.

But whatever your photo suggestion may be, make absolutely certain you are prepared before you invite newspaper and television camera people. *PR News* tells a story about Tom Womack and a campaign he worked on while at Burson-Martsteller for American Airlines, which involved a media event and a photo shoot at Dallas/Ft. Worth Airport. The only problem? Well . . . everything.

"We needed to shoot at DFW plus there was a third-party vendor involved," Womack told *PR News*. "There was not a clearly delineated line of responsibility."

Womack's photo shoot never happened because of too many complicating factors, and it is a prime example of how PR practitioners—on both agency and corporate sides—need to be prepared when it comes to orchestrating shoots for anything from headshots to brochures for a client's product launch. Problems often arise when the PR practitioner is too far removed from the situation or does not play a large enough role in planning, and leaves things to an out-of-house photographer, a camera-shy CEO, or—worse-case scenario—a combination of both.

No matter now many precautions you take, there is never a guarantee that a photo shoot will go according to your plans. The newspaper's photographer or television cameraman may have different ideas. Your suggestions will still help.

I agree with what has been said for a long time: A picture is worth a thousand words and can convey a point more effective than words.

WEEKLY NEWSPAPERS

Local weekly community newspapers are the easiest media targets for your story. Often, they are sadly forgotten when one is thinking of publicity.

I ran my own weekly newspaper in the Hamptons resort area outside of New York City for several years and wrote for a chain of weeklies in Florida.

People that came to us with tips and story ideas were the lifeline of our business. And the ones who came to us arrogantly, couldn't spell, or didn't know our names, never got to first base with us.

Weeklies are usually read cover to cover. The first thing you should do is gather copies of all the weeklies in your area and study them. Learn the key names. Don't write a pitch letter that begins "Dear Editor." Write "Dear Mr. Jones" (or Mrs. Jones, Ms. Jones).

Your press release or pitch letter should be basically the same as the one you are writing for the big daily, except you can write with a local angle.

The biggest plus about landing a good story in a weekly is the merchandising you can do after publication. First and foremost, the weekly newspaper that has published the story acts as a third-party endorsement. Reprint the article (you should get permission from the publication because the material is copyrighted, though many do not ask for permission) and distribute it to your customers, potential customers, suppliers, and anyone else important to your business.

Editors and writers for the daily newspapers in your area read the weeklies and get story ideas from them. When I had my weekly in New York, the managing editor of the daily newspaper *Newsday* took me to lunch one day and offered his help if I ever needed it. He said he couldn't afford to put a staff reporter in my area and he read my paper every week to see what was going on there.

Don't underestimate weekly newspapers. When I worked for the *Lake Worth Herald,* a small weekly located in central Palm Beach County, Florida. I wrote one story about a simple account of a bomb threat at my local post office—which earlier was the pass-through station for a letter containing anthrax that ultimately killed a *National Enquirer* photo editor. That article and several more I wrote were picked up and posted on *www.postalwatch.org*, a post office watchdog Web site. I started hearing from postal workers from all over the country and ended up writing 68 articles about horrific stories within the U.S. Postal Service.

I wrote a series of articles about the USPS's sponsorship of Lance Armstrong's cycling team and the wasteful spending of tens of millions of dollars.

My series, in this small weekly newspaper, led to a USPS inspector general's investigation of the post office sponsorship program. The Office of Inspector General report moved the USPS to cancel its sponsorship of the Lance Armstrong team.

NEWSLETTERS

Years ago, when newsletters weren't as popular as they are today, I created one for my client Johnson & Johnson (J&J) for its baby products. J&J owned the baby-marketing space for baby shampoo, baby oil, and baby powder. Because no one else was marketing these products, I did not have to publicize trademarked names.

Therefore, I created the Health and Beauty Newsletter. The majority of items in the newsletter were common tips on promoting good health and finding beauty. Items relating to the benefits of J&J's baby products were sprinkled throughout the newsletter. "For a healthy and good looking sun tan, try a little baby oil . . ." J& J's name was never mentioned in the newsletter.

Most newsletters are published mainly for customers and prospects, but my J&J newsletter was strictly a PR tactic. We mailed the newsletter to thousands of weekly and daily newspaper editors who focused on health and beauty. The results were amazing and assured my client a leadership position in baby products for decades to come.

Publishing a printed or online newsletter is a tactic that can ensure consistent exposure to target audiences even in a market that is saturated with all kinds of newsletters and blogs.

Newsletters can be distributed online, which drastically cuts costs from a printed and mailed version. A newsletter can be a sales marketing or PR tool or both. Target audiences can include the media, customers, and prospects. A regularly published newsletter keeps your name in front of your key audiences and is certainly cheaper than advertising.

To see a few examples of online newsletters, go to *www. newsletteraccess.com,* which lists some 10,000 newsletters, many free, covering a wide variety of topics.

To begin a newsletter, first develop the newsletter design, then work on scheduling and figuring out what to write about. And after all that, you still have to write every issue.

The frequency of a newsletter depends on your ability to come up with good material. Your readers will label your newsletter junk mail if the content isn't fresh and newsy. If you have the material, I recommend you publish no more than six issues a year, though it's probably best to limit the frequency to three or four annually. Many small business owners, organizations, and nonprofit groups start newsletters as a way to keep in touch with their target audiences. But they soon find themselves completely overwhelmed with all the work.

Newsletter content can talk about everything new going on in the company, such as products, campaigns, employees. Human interest stories about customers or employees are always good. Case histories and milestones in your company or organization's history work nicely. Remember, a picture is worth a thousand words. Don't use head shots of key people; try and get pictures of them at work (or play) or using a new product. Never use a photo of subjects lined up, or as I call it, a firing line picture. A letter from a CEO, president, or key executive is good, but don't make them too wordy.

A newsletter is a good way to merchandise any print or broadcast publicity you have obtained. If you were not successful in placing your press release, you can publish it in your newsletter. Highlights of speeches made by your key players work well. Keep the excerpts short.

There are many newsletters available that will help the do-it-your-selfer or small PR firm. Among the best I found is *Bill Stoller's Free Publicity, The Newsletter for PR-Hungry Businesses*. Stoller has spent two decades in public relations including stints with Burson-Marsteller and Cohn & Wolfe.

I asked Stoller to describe his mission. "We have one goal: to help businesses and individuals obtain publicity without spending a fortune. We believe that anyone, with some perseverance, direction, and good advice, can generate substantial coverage in newspapers, magazines, radio, and TV," Stoller told me. Stoller's newsletter offers editorial calendars, specific needs of top editors, and Internet PR secrets.

10

HOW TO STAGE MANAGE
THE INTERVIEW
Don't Blow It Now

Okay, your lead is terrific. The editor reads through your one-page release and passes it to one of his reporters to do a story. The reporter telephones you to set up an interview. You got the newspaper's interest by writing a clear and concise brief. You don't want to blow it when the reporter calls.

Reporters, like all media professionals, respond to good interviewees. They give good interviewees more attention and great credence. So it is vital that interview subjects handle the give-and-take with coolness, authority, and ease. An interview is like a Broadway show; it can be a big hit or a bomb. The PR professional is the impresario, or, if you're acting as your own counsel, you're the director and star.

The interview is a trade-off. The interviewee wants something: personal publicity; attention to a cause; promotion for a product, service, or business; or a third-party endorsement for election or reelection. The interviewer wants something as well: facts for a story, confirmation of a rumor, or conflict with another point of view. This chapter tells you the tactics public relations pros use to produce hit interviews. If you're a do-it-yourselfer, read slowly and carefully. If you are a PR practitioner, read slowly and carefully.

The more interviews you do, the better you will become. When Jim Buckley was elected U.S. Senator from New York, I went to Washington with him as his press secretary. Buckley was the opposite of a spin doctor—quiet and somewhat shy. But when you got to know him, you loved him. The first thing I did for him was start a weekly press breakfast (the media brought the doughnuts, we supplied the coffee) in the senator's office. Every Tuesday morning, except for holidays and when the senator was traveling, he met with the New York press. Oftentimes, national press members would drop by. No senator from New York had ever been this accessible to the media. He got so used to meeting with the media, it wasn't a chore for him any longer. The media hailed Buckley for his openness whether they personally agreed or disagreed with his positions. They learned he was not a bomb thrower. The Tuesday-morning crowd talked to their colleagues in the press galleries and bars throughout Washington. It would cause the *Washington Post*'s David Broder, probably the best political reporter in the country to this day, and certainly not a conservative Republican, to say that Buckley was one of the nicest and smartest men ever to serve in the Senate.

ARE YOU ONE OF THESE?

Steve Cody and Jenny Grendel have trained hundreds of executives over the years in their positions as managing partner and senior account executive, respectively, of Peppercoy, a New York–based strategic communications firm.

They are struck by how many executives struggle to explain their organization, mission, and points of differentiation.

"In our post-Enron world, investors are holding top executives strictly accountable for their public proclamations, to the point where a CEO's blunder could drastically affect an organization's reputation, share price, and bottom line," say Cody and Grendel.

Cody and Grendel categorized most executives in one of three ways for *Bulldog Reporter's Barks and Bites* online newsletter:

The Boardroom Speaker: Constantly using corporate jargon. Organizational mumbo jumbo may be understood within the confines of the business, but it leaves the general public (and investors) totally baffled.

The Salesman: Always focused on "closing the deal" and turns a media interview into a 60-second commercial.

The Charmer: Tries to become fast friends with the reporter in hopes that it will result in a positive story.

Obviously, you don't want to be like one of these people.

IT'S INTERVIEW TIME

When an interview is slated, interviewee and PR professional, if there is one, should prepare thoroughly. Obviously the time and place should be pinned down. It can take place in your store, office, or maybe your home. Many interviewees have supreme confidence in their ability to think on their feet and handle tough questions. Nevertheless, it is important that there be a briefing session with the PR professional. If you're working on your own, these tips will help.

If the interview is on television, the interviewee should know how to—and how not to—dress. There are no strict rules. At one time people going on television avoided wearing white because it tended to glare on the screen, but due to improved television equipment, that isn't a concern today. In most cases, dress is pretty much a matter of taste. It is not an audience with the pope; the interviewee need not dress with excessive sobriety. However, busy patterns do not usually work well except in small doses, as in a tie or scarf. Dark suits and jackets usually look better than lighter ones. Dresses of one predominant color, offset by contrasting colors, are often better than garments of many colors.

If visual materials—charts, graphs, products, and photos—are important to the interview, they must be furnished to the interviewer beforehand.

The idea of the interview is to convey a certain message or messages. Write them down and study them. Here are a few examples:

- This is an important new development.
- Our new product is the best on the market.
- The new retail business is unique.
- The company is carrying out its responsibilities.
- We are succeeding and growing.

If the interview is for print, read things the interviewer has written. Form an impression of the interviewer's style if you can. Thoughtful? Colorful? Funny? Knowing what the interviewer is like does not mean that the subject should go to great lengths to change his or her own style.

Once the objectives have been identified, prepare to work them into answers. Come up with a list of the questions that are likely to be asked—starting with the toughest. The interviewee may protest, "That is not a fair question . . . I am not going to get into that. . . ." There is nothing in the rules that says the interviewer must ask fair questions. No question can be ruled out. And there is no way to control what will be asked.

Interviewees should go into the interview with a positive frame of mind. Remember, the interview is a forum and an opportunity. Interviewees should not worry about not being asked the right question. They should give a prepared answer to a question that is somewhere in the ballpark. Good interviewees are adept at answering the questions they like, rather than the questions they were asked. Interviewees should give a brief answer to a question in the same general area and then bridge to the desired information they want to get out. For example, "In that connection, I might add that along with the crystal beads, we will be selling. . . ."

Another way an interviewee can cover points is to volunteer material. Responding to the question, the interviewee can say, "There are two answers to that. Before I get to them, there is something I forgot to mention before. . . ." Give the volunteered answer quickly, and then answer the original question.

It is a good idea to preface an answer with a headline that encapsulates the point, and then elaborate. The elaboration should contain quotable facts and figures. Even more important, it should contain, if possible, usable anecdotes. Anecdotes are meat and drink to journalists. Have a lot of them and sprinkle them through the interview. If the interviewer doesn't end up with good anecdotes and good quotes, there's usually no story.

If pictures can be used to illustrate a story, they should be given to the newspaper or magazine. Black-and-white glossies or color prints are preferred, and, of course, digital photos are widely used now. Shots usually should include people, even in product photos. Only design engineers drool with delight over unadorned pictures of machines. The interviewer might be given a selection of shots of the interviewee. Candid, informal shots are usually better than formal portraits. Sizes of photos can vary—eventually they will be cropped and changed in size. It is best to provide pictures that are larger than necessary. Small pictures become grainy when they are blown up. Among the most popular sizes are 4" × 5" and 5" × 7".

GROUND RULES

Certain executives think PR practitioners can prevent unwelcome questions: "I am not prepared to answer, so tell them not to ask that one." If certain questions are really tricky, or if the interviewee is unwilling to deal with them, then the interview should be scrubbed.

"No comment" is not a satisfactory response. Nor is, "I will have my people get back to you." Corporate leaders are used to dealing in broad strokes while having subordinates work out details. In a press interview, particularly a TV interview, the interviewee does not have this luxury. Interviewers will understand that the interviewee does not have command of every detail, but he or she must be able to talk about significant details.

Some interviewees want strict ground rules. Interviewers do not like to be fenced in by ground rules. Furthermore, if ground rules are forced on an interviewer, that person may become antagonistic. An antagonistic interviewer has many ways to make a interviewee look bad. It is far better to work hard to get the interviewee ready to handle hard questions.

Obviously, an interview that is broadcast live is the riskiest. But the interviewee should not develop a false sense of security because an interview is being taped. The plus side to the live interview is that you can get your point across with no fear of it being edited out.

When an interviewee is accompanied by a public relations professional, the PR professional can be of some help, but not all that much. Media professionals do not usually like it when PR practitioners come to the interview as keepers. At an interview, the PR practitioner should speak only when spoken to.

BEING PREPARED IS NOT JUST FOR BOY SCOUTS

Before an interview, remember: Rehearse, rehearse, rehearse. It's hard to get busy, important people to rehearse an interview. They are likely to say, "Give me a list of the questions, and I will go over them." That is not good enough. On television and radio, how interviewees behave themselves can be as significant as what they say. And, while the circumstances are different, the same goes for a newspaper or magazine interview.

So, there should be a pull-no-punches rehearsal where questions are asked and are answered. The best kind of rehearsal for a TV interview may be one in which a mock interview is videotaped and played back. Using this technique, people who think they are answering questions cogently and interestingly might discover, to their chagrin, that they actually come across as incomprehensible, wooden, long-winded, and evasive.

REMAIN COOL

Sometimes an interviewer may appear hostile because of the interviewer's style. Mike Wallace, Bill O'Reilly, Tim Russert, Don Imus, and similar personalities have made aggressive questioning a high-rated TV art form; in the hands of certain interviewers, it is a short step from aggressiveness to hostility.

Sometimes the interviewer may be aggressive and confrontational because the situation calls for it. The subject may be a candidate running for the local town council. The interviewer brings up something derogatory about him and he now has to answer the charges. The interviewee is not prepared to comment on something that the interviewer wants to hear about.

Occasionally, an interviewer seems to become—at least to the subject—aggressive and hostile for no reason at all. This can happen because the subject mishandles the process and makes the interviewer angry. An angry interviewer can, with a smile, make an amateurish subject look very bad.

Here are some suggestions for interviewees when the atmosphere is stormy.

Remain detached and unemotional. By far the best thing to do when confronted with hostility is to pause, breathe in slowly, and answer unemotionally. When subjects blow their cool, they put themselves in the hands of the interviewer.

After remaining calm, the next challenge for the interviewee is to respond to a hostile question without showing anger or turning the interview into a shootout. Here are some answers to avoid:

- "You've got that all wrong."
- "I strongly disagree with you."
- "You haven't got your facts straight."
- "That's all wrong, and I'm going to tell you why."
- "Where did you get that idea?"

The trick is to avoid addressing the interviewer as "you" in a negative way or confrontational sense. It is much better to make it positive, such as:

- "You raise an interesting point. Let's look at it."
- "You state the problem very well. I'd like to tell you how it's being solved."
- "You've identified an issue that many people have raised. In part, they're correct; in part, they're incorrect. Let's look at the issue."

There is one advantage to a skeptical, aggressive interview. The subject gets a chance to restate the desired message, with appropriate variations. A well-delivered message, in the context of hostile questions, gains credibility. The idea is for the subject to calmly insist on his or her points without restating the critic's position. Restating the oppositional point of view just gives it more credibility and attention.

An interviewer may become impatient if the subject covers the same ground. The subject, refusing to be flustered, can say, "Because we seem to have some misunderstanding here, don't you want me to try to clear it up?"

SOME TIPS

Snappy interjections of humor and flip remarks are dangerous. They may go well at a meeting or in a speech before a friendly and familiar audience, but in an interview with a broadcast or print reporter, interviewees should leave humor alone. It can backfire. The interviewee can look calloused or frivolous. Worse (and this happens with dismaying frequency), what is meant as a joke is taken seriously.

At times, experienced interviewers use a ploy that isn't a question. It is nothing at all—a pregnant pause. For example, a subject gives a short, effective answer to a touchy question. The interviewer says nothing. The subject begins to sweat. The dead air is oppressive. Finally, the subject blurts out an additional explanation, which usually seems weak and apologetic.

When a TV interviewer pauses, the interviewee should simply sit and think about questions that are likely to come up next. The dead air is the host's responsibility, not the subject's. The subject should look at the host with a calm, expectant smile. The camera should show the subject's cool, confident face.

The interviewee should jot down likely questions on index cards and rehearse alone in front of a mirror. A tape recorder is handy; by listening to the answers, the subject can refine the answers to make them crisp and more persuasive.

After the interview ends, the PR practitioner's work continues. The first follow-up step is to find out when the interview (if it was taped) will run. Alert employees, customers, prospects, suppliers, and everyone else you know. Use the TV interview as a learning experience; analyze, discuss, and figure out how to do even better the next time.

For a print interview, make sure your target audiences receives a copy. If you have a Web site, post the print interview as well as radio and television interviews.

11

NEWS CONFERENCES
Build It and They Might Not Come

Have you heard the story about the public relations practitioner who held a news conference and no one came? It happened to me once, and it happens more and more in these days of new-age public relations. When a reporter has the Internet and Web casts, why should he or she leave the office?

The first question to ask about a news conference is whether to have one. Some clients think the answer is simple. Because a news conference appears more important than sending out a release, clients feel their PR professionals should always arrange conferences whenever there is anything they want in print or on the air.

Wrong. The tool is a *news* conference, not a *con* conference. The worst use of a news conference is to call reporters together and then con them into running a nonstory that is simply a puff for the client's point of view. Those who see these occasions as opportunities for spin or manipulation often refer to them as press conferences. We should stick to the term *news* conference as a semantic reminder that solid meat must be served to the media.

The news conference at one time was a staple item of public relations. Even today, when used well, it gets stories used and wins friends in the media.

It is also a production, aimed at a tough audience. To get the desired response from this audience, PR professionals must ensure that the production is well managed. This means the spokespeople should be well rehearsed, the props should be ready, and the production should run smoothly.

DON'T TRY THIS

The most successful news conference I ever held was during Watergate when I worked for Senator Jim Buckley. I had to get media people to a news conference where Senator Buckley was to announce his call for President Nixon's resignation. However, I couldn't give them a clue about what was going to happen for fear the White House would learn about it in advance and try to persuade the senator to postpone the conference. I put out a news alert the day before that read:

Senator James Buckley (R-NY) will hold a news conference on Watergate in the Senate Caucus Room at 10 AM, Wednesday March 19 (1974).

Short and sweet. (Don't even think of trying it today; the media won't stand for not knowing in advance what they have been asked to cover.) The phones started ringing. What was Buckley up to? Was the conference worth attending? The television people reminded me of what I already knew—there were only so many TV crews available. They couldn't assign a three-person crew unless they thought the news was worthy of being broadcast on network news.

I told everyone that I could not divulge the contents of the Buckley statement, but I put my reputation and credibility on the line by assuring them I believed it would make the top of their newscasts. In my six years on Capitol Hill, I never could have been accused of spin, and that stood me in good stead in this case.

Buckley's statement calling for President Nixon's resignation would be big news considering he would be the first Republican to call for the president's resignation. This was heresy for a man who had seconded Nixon's nomination at the Republican Convention in Miami two years earlier.

Fifteen minutes before the conference was to start, the historic caucus room was overflowing with reporters, camera crews, and broadcasting equipment.

About two minutes before I was to walk Buckley to the conference, I received a call from Carl Leubsdorf, then the Capitol Hill reporter for the Associated Press, who told me he was going to write that Buckley was going to call for Nixon's resignation. "Would I be wrong?" he asked. I knew it was a ploy reporters sometimes used to try to find out something. In any event, given the hour, I had no fear of the White House intervening. And besides, helping out the AP was good for the future. I told him to go with the story. He put a flash on the AP wire and seconds later it was read in the White House. When I picked up Buckley to take him to the news conference, his secretary told me that General Alexander Haig, Nixon's chief of staff, was calling. I told Buckley's secretary to tell Haig that the senator had already left.

Buckley would later describe the few hundred yards to the news conference room as "the longest walk of my political life."

Buckley dropped his bombshell. The three television networks all led with the story, using a combined total of 40 minutes, and nearly every newspaper in the country gave it prominent attention on their front pages.

I'M NOT PERFECT

Even delivering solid meat at a news conference doesn't always work to perfection. In 2005, I was representing an organization in Lake Worth, Florida, that was campaigning against a referendum that was coming up for a vote in a week. I scheduled a news conference in front of a decaying house (good visual) under foreclosure whose sale would be affected by a positive vote. No one showed up except the editor of the *Lake Worth Herald*, the local weekly newspaper. The reporter for the daily *Palm Beach Post* called me by cell phone to tell me she got tied up. I let her talk to some of the principals by phone and hand delivered some material. The news conference wasn't a total failure, but came very close without the presence of important television and radio representatives, one of the main reasons you hold a news conference in the first place.

IS THE NEWS SUBSTANTIAL?

What constitutes news? When an organization is involved in a big, ongoing story, almost any statement of substance by a top officer is news. Unfortunately, such ongoing stories are usually negative—there is a problem, scandal, or disaster.

If the logic of the news conference is not dictated by a general situation, then somebody must decide whether the desired message is substantial enough to warrant a full-blown news conference. Perhaps it should be disseminated via some other means. This decision should be made by a PR professional or a PR-savvy individual and no one else. Public relations professionals and all others should put themselves in the shoes of reporters, editors, and broadcast news directors and ask, "What's in this for me?" If a cold-blooded, objective answer says the story lacks sufficient appeal or will be seen just as a plug, then the decision should be *no conference.*

New developments constitute news. A new product or service is news. It is big news to the organization, and probably, pretty big news to the industry. But is it big enough that you want to ask a reporter to leave his or her office to hear you talk about it? Can it be handled by sending out press materials?

One of my clients, Philip Morris, loved news conferences. At one time, they were releasing results of a survey about women for Virginia Slims cigarettes. They wanted to hold a news conference. That was business-as-usual procedure. I told them, in this case, the media would appreciate it if we just sent them the survey. We did. Reporters who had questions simply called me or the contact people at Philip Morris. The coverage was excellent, perhaps even better than if we had held a news conference.

If you're calling a news conference just to seek attention, I strongly recommend you forget about it. Some years ago, a little-read magazine published an article called "The 10 Dumbest Congressmen." The piece listed the exploits of the ten individuals. A U.S. senator from Virginia was singled out as the dumbest—Number One. The senator was understandably outraged. And to vent his wrath, two days after the article's publication, he called a press conference to deny that he was "the single dumbest congressman," thus proving the article's point. After his press conference, the world knew who was the dumbest of them all.

NEWS BRIEFINGS WORK

If the topic does not warrant a full-blown news conference, but is worth more than a release, a news briefing is a good alternative. A news briefing is less formal and confrontational. It is usually held off premises, often in a hotel meeting room or suite. For my client Michelin Tire, who was introducing the *Michelin Florida Tourist Guide,* I invited the news media to lunch at a new swanky hotel in South Beach, part of Miami Beach. The informality of the occasion made it more social than a formal presentation. The Michelin lunch was highly successful and resulted in good coverage for the guide book.

BEFORE THE CONFERENCE

If a full-scale news conference is the best way to get the message out, a number of logistical questions must be addressed.

Rent a meeting room in a hotel with a convenient location—convenient for the media, not for the people holding the conference. It is best to stay away from private clubs unless it is a press club. Clubs (university or otherwise) may convey an elitist image. And some clubs are regarded as discriminatory against women or minorities. Maybe that inference is inaccurate and unfair; maybe whatever discrimination that existed in the past has been banished. It does not matter. Don't take a chance. The location should not be a potential problem in any way.

Arrange chairs facing a low-rise platform with a dais. Make provisions for television and radio; there should be ample electrical facilities. If necessary, obtain a mult box from the hotel or communications supplier that permits many recorders to be plugged in and the spokesperson to speak from only one microphone.

There is a notion in some quarters that reporters at a news conference should be supplied with food and drinks. This may go back to the stereotype that these ink-stained wretches are always starved for a decent meal, and that they are inveterate boozers. Even if this were the case—and it is not—the conference should not take place at a meal, nor should it be a party with an open bar. (Parties for the media have their place, but not at a news conference.) The event should be crisp and businesslike, respecting the time demands on the reporters and conveying the idea that this is an important event.

Not that the event should be Spartan. There should be a table at the back with good, hot coffee and hot water, tea bags, and maybe doughnuts. I say doughnuts because a midmorning news conference is usually best. The convenience of the media is all-important when deciding on a time for a news conference. A mid- to late-morning news conference is usually best. It makes the evening news, and it lets reporters write their stories for the next day's papers without a rush.

Press parties are quite different from news conferences. These are *parties,* put together to introduce the media to an organization, a company, or people in the organization. The food and drink should be first-rate. There should be no effort to cover serious topics. The party is a tool that should be used only on appropriate, light-hearted occasions . . . when you can afford the good food and drink. While you might get some coverage, don't expect it. The press party is usually an investment in the future.

INVITING THE PRESS

The announcement or advisory of the news conference should be mailed and e-mailed, if possible, to all appropriate media. Except in unusual circumstances, it should be addressed to the broadcast news directors or editors rather than reporters. Let the editors assign reporters. Editors rightfully resent usurpation of that function. Besides giving the time, place, and sponsor of the news conference, the announcement should—unless it is obvious— tell what is going to be presented. This is a *sell* document; media professionals have to be sold on devoting their time to the conference. If there will be good visuals, other than people, include this in the alert. Follow up with telephone calls the day before, and the morning of, the conference.

Reporters will ask, "What is your person going to say?" Don't respond, "Show up and you'll hear it." Unless the news value is obvious, you must give media representatives a reason for attending. What I did with Senator Buckley was an exception to this rule. The more important the media, the greater the sales resistance.

Don't guarantee a great story. If there is doubt as to whether there will be a story for the major media, then the organizer should be candid about it.

If you have a press kit, it should help reporters write their stories. It should contain the opening statement of the spokesperson, biographies of all participants and relevant people, background material, photos, and any other relevant information. Distribute the kits at the news conference.

Rehearse before the news conference. Make sure the lights and microphones work, all visuals are present and operative, computers and Internet connections have been checked, and there are no bugs. Media people notice whether a news conference is run well or badly. A professionally run event denotes professionalism all along the line. An amateurish news conference is harmful. It can erode credibility. It can have an unconscious effect on those attending. Even if the content is solid, sloppy packaging tarnishes the perception.

The conference should start with an opening statement. This statement must be carefully crafted. It will lay out the essentials of the message. The written statement should be handed out at the beginning. The spokespeople should be well rehearsed, of course, and part of that rehearsal must be emphasis on the role of the statement. First of all, the opening statement does not set the ground rules. Reporters may ask questions that have little or nothing to do with the topics covered in the statement. This is particularly true if the organization is involved in newsworthy activities that are not covered in the statement. There should be no ground rules for the media.

USING TECHNOLOGY

Everything in this chapter so far has explained how PR practitioners have been holding news conferences for years, and still do, this author included. However, technology experts have added considerably to what can be done with a news conference, and these additions should be considered.

Jim Sulley has 25 years of experience in news and PR and is one of those experts who is adding new dimensions to news conferences. He is a senior vice president in charge of operations at Newscast, a specialist in visual communications aimed at today's media.

"When it comes to putting on news conferences, many PR professionals are still living in the Stone Age. It's no secret that the way the media delivers stories has changed dramatically over the past few years," Sulley says.

But surprisingly, most news conferences are conducted in the same manner they were 25 years ago. Communications specialists must adapt to and approach news conferences in ways that will enable them to provide today's news organizations with story elements demanded by the new Internet age, according to Sulley in an interview he gave to the *Bulldog Reporter's Barks and Bytes*.

The Web has transformed traditional media. The *New York Times* now offers video on a daily basis to its online readers. The *Washington Post*, the *Rocky Mountain News*, and others now use "flash journalism"—pictures, video, and audio integrated into an interactive package that lets online readers view the story as they want in the order they want.

Journalists now face the challenge of changing how they gather the elements of their stories—at many newspapers, photographers are expected to gather audio and shoot video, in addition to providing traditional photos.

And many radio and TV sites are making greater use of pictures and video as part of multimedia packages every day.

These changes create new opportunities for communications professionals who can help journalists gather these new story elements—particularly at news conferences. In doing so, communications pros can improve the depth and impact of media coverage.

Following are a few excellent tips from Sulley for maximizing opportunities around news conferences in the changing world of Web-based media:

- Provide visual opportunities beyond people simply speaking at the podium
- If the event is about a new product, provide working units for the media
- Make key participants available after the event for interviews and demonstrations
- Make sure everyone is miked (especially for the Q&A, which often generates the best audio)
- Provide a mult box with plenty of outlets to meet the media's increased need to caption audio
- Give the media equal opportunity to gather the parts of the story they need; don't favor the larger media outlets over the smaller print and Web-based ones
- Realize the way news is gathered has changed; a photographer requesting sound bites might seem odd, but many traditional print outlets now post audio online
- Provide a clean line of site to the stage, and ample room for equipment
- Provide interesting visual opportunities; good visual stories get the most play

While some of these tips may seem obvious, many of the basics of a news conference are not followed. With the changes taking place in the media—and the way they gather stories—these steps become even more important.

Although we are seeing a dramatic media transformation, the basic goal of news conferences has not changed. If the media does not come away with compelling and interesting story elements—video, photos, and audio, in addition to the story itself—the coverage is likely to be disappointing.

12

SURVEYS, SURVEYS, SURVEYS
Measuring Public Opinion

Ned Hubbell, who recently retired as an instructor in public relations at the University of Michigan, spent 26 years conducting opinion research. To prepare you for a chapter on the subjects of surveys and research, here's an example from Hubbell's own experience that will make your mind start working . . . fast.

The manager of a rock-and-roll radio station hired my firm to do an opinion survey of listeners' music preferences. The survey revealed that people in his market area preferred country & western. When he saw the results, he was appalled. Personally, he disliked country & western. He said there must have been something wrong with my sampling.

About a year later, after his ratings kept slipping, he asked me to do the survey again. This time, the results came back even stronger for country & western. Based on that research, he reluctantly changed formats—and his ratings shot through the roof.

In the current era of pollsters and instant market research, conducting surveys about interesting and controversial topics has become one of the most powerful communications tools available. Simply put, the media love data. We live in a *USA Today*, 24/7 news world, in which every issue can be unveiled in a snapshot. Tying a statistic to a story can make the story come alive. Whether it's a fashionable, expensive survey or something properly executed by one person, the use of surveys in company, product, and cause-related public relations is a potent force for telling a story.

After an important election was held in Lake Worth, Florida, and only 15 percent of the registered voters participated, I suggested to interested political groups the first thing they should do is conduct a survey of all voters to find out why they didn't vote.

SURVEYS FOR PUBLICITY PURPOSES

In communications, research means in-depth interviews; focus groups; convenience polls; mail and phone surveys; analysis of customer records, industry trends, and news clippings; and so on, according to Mark Holoweiko, a principal in StonyPoint Communications, a leading marketing and PR firm in Michigan.

As Holoweiko puts it:

> Certain CEOs and public relations practitioners sour at the suggestion of spending time or money on research.
>
> These otherwise sensible people apparently believe that because they know their business, they automatically know the answer to their communications problems. In other words, "Don't confuse me with the facts. My mind is made up."

The bottom line: The aim of communications research is to open a kind of dialogue with key publics or audiences such as customers, employees, voters, members, contributors, or whoever.

Public relations is a potent force for telling a story.

Organizations can use surveys to promote links between topics and products, and establish organizational credibility. A survey can subtly promote a product's assets, a political candidate's experience, or the need for a particular service without ever naming a brand. If a survey of mothers says a telephone call is the best present they can get for Mother's Day, phone companies will want to get that information out.

As another example, a florist might conduct a survey of women's preferences for flowers on Valentine's Day.

At the Richard Weiner agency, we conducted what we called a minisurvey using one question only four words long. We asked *Fortune 500* chief executive officers, "How tall are you?" The answers showed that the majority of CEOs are over six feet tall. The results, quoted by the Weiner client, made the front page of the *Wall Street Journal.*

If a survey is conducted for publicity purposes, it is critical that the data be valid. Ironically, although the media may often publish data that is suspect, PR and research professionals understand and expect that the samples used are representative and honest, and that the results accurately describe the entire population sampled. CNN and other network and cable stations often ask viewers to vote on an issue. The results make their newscasts but are far from scientifically accurate.

Like any marketing/public relations communications campaign, if the program goals are clear at the outset, the results will be more compelling and so will the conclusions that can be drawn from them. Use surveys to focus on needs, advantages, or unique distinctions, or to confirm the proven popularity of a product, service, cause, preference, or need.

Know your communications objectives, including the messages you would like to convey, your strategy for conveying them, and the target audience you want to reach. All of these insights will help you focus the research, survey the right populations, and design the questionnaire in a way that will elicit the kind of response you seek.

Select and commit your resources according to your budget, time pressure, and the kind of scrutiny you expect to undergo. All research must be sound and statistically valid.

Before you embark on a survey, it's important to know what's already been said about a subject. It is also important to know how to exploit the opportunities of what has not quite been said about a subject.

Let's say you own a hardware store; you have a new battery-operated lamp in stock and you want to sell in areas that might be hit hardest in hurricane season.

The first thing you can do is to go to the search engines—Google, Yahoo, Microsoft, Ask.com—and type in *hurricanes;* the search results should give you insight as to what's going on to help you develop a minisurvey.

As with any research, the questionnaire must be phrased with precision. When you are producing a survey whose results you want to use for publicity purposes, how you phrase the question is often more important than the topic itself.

The style of the question you ask can influence your results. Open-ended questions are more difficult to tabulate but can provide excellent sound bites. Although verbatim results occasionally give valuable and printable color commentary, they can also become an unwieldy volume of wide-ranging personal opinions that are more trouble than they are worth to interpret for a general audience. In contrast, ratings and ranking questions (e.g., "On a scale of 1 to 5 . . ." or "Rank the following from first to last . . .") are useful strategies that will generate good comparative data from which to make claims and give authoritative insights.

Carefully think about the exact nature of the responses you seek. To be certain your questions lead you to the desired response, construct the questions backward, beginning with your desired response. Then pretest the survey by fielding it as a pilot among a limited sample group. If preliminary results go the wrong way or if the answers to questions will refute other points you are trying to make through the survey, then kill or change the problematic questions. Unsavory response data cannot be hidden if the integrity of the entire survey is to stand, so pretest it first. Research rules mandate that you must provide the full set of data if the media request it.

After sending information to the media, the provider should expect to answer all sorts of probing questions. And the provider should welcome such inquiries. Provide the research methodology, the questionnaire instrument, and the survey results to anyone who requests them. For the survey results to have an impact, the provider must stand by them and defend their credibility. Offering interpretation of the data via quotes allows you to pull out the most critical points for your perspective and to ensure they are not overlooked.

By supplementing a press release about the data with graphic interpretations of some of the most exciting findings, you can increase the chances of the results being picked up. Distribute camera-ready illustrations of data highlights as charts and graphs. Identify the source of the information (i.e., you or your client) directly in the prepared illustration, making it easy for publications to give the credit in ink.

Bob Seltzer is a true believer of using surveys in public relations. First as a top executive of Richard Weiner and Porter Novelli, then as president and chief executive officer of Ogilvy Public Relations Worldwide, and now as leader of the Marketing Practice at Ruder & Finn, Seltzer lists surveys as one of the major tools in the public relations mix:

A good survey can lay the foundation for a replenishing supply of future publicity. It can become a bench mark against which results from the same survey in future years can be compared.

This evergreen situation yields consistent publicity by using a platform that, by repeating it annually, builds on its own credibility. It also can serve to give the sponsoring organization associated with it a strong hold on future discussion regarding the topic. Surveys that generate publicity and credibility are ones that have fulfilled their promise.

If you haven't gotten your feet wet, maybe now is a good time to jump into the survey waters. And remember, surveys can be as short and simple as you want them to be.

For credibility, you should align with an independent organization. If your research conclusions on behalf of your business or client speak favorably about the business or product, it is likely to look suspicious and self-serving. But if a recognized research organization is responsible for finding the same data, this lends third-party objectivity to the research and assures the media that even if it is self-serving, it is still credible. By aligning with an outside firm, public relations practitioners and their clients have the validity of an independent brand to back up their data.

You can choose from many tactical formats for surveys, depending on your budget, time line, and the depth of information you expect to receive from your respondents. Research firms conduct weekly and nightly omnibus surveys that poll general population samples, usually by telephone or in mall intercepts, using an assortment of collected questions from firms seeking to measure public opinion about numerous specific topics. If you ask the right questions and insert your specific queries in these regularly conducted surveys, it will only cost a few thousand dollars and can yield immediate, valid results.

On the other hand, creating your own custom questionnaire and fielding an in-depth survey will likely yield a richer body of data and allow you to more substantially examine the issues that can be used to fuel and perpetuate marketing campaigns.

Creative Research Systems, a Petaluma, California–based software firm that provides software for researchers, offers a good list of seven steps in a survey project on its Web site at *www.surveysystem.com:*

1. Establish the goals of the project—what you want to learn
2. Determine your sample—who you will interview
3. Choose interviewing methodology—how you will interview
4. Create your questionnaire—what you will ask
5. Pretest the questionnaire, if practical—test the questions
6. Conduct interviews and enter data—ask the questions
7. Analyze the data—produce the reports

WebSurveyer's Michelle McCann and Meg Walker say you probably have tons of new story ideas hidden inside your own company. "The best way to uncover these buried gems is to survey your customers. How do they feel about 2006–2007? What is their economic outlook for the years ahead?" The results of a customer survey can make a good news story and will give credence to one's position as a thought leader.

With the increasing importance of return on investment and accountability, research has emerged with more significance than ever before.

David Rockland, partner and global director of research at the Ketchum PR firm, told *PR Week* in July 2005 the agency's research division grew more than threefold in the past five years. "We have seen a desire by clients to know their target better," he said. "PR has become more a rifle-shot business as opposed to shotgun. The relationship between research and PR has become stronger."

There is a place for research and surveys in a budget, even if you have to accomplish the mission yourself.

13

CRISIS COMMUNICATIONS

What to Do If Disaster Strikes

Public relations isn't all leisurely planning and fun and games. If a crisis suddenly erupts, it's a big mistake not to be ready.

Crisis means victims, catastrophe, and explosive visibility. A crisis could be a natural disaster, a scandal, a sabotage, or a terrorist attack. People at the top of a business or organization need trusted advisors who can help them deal with a crisis situation.

Having a crisis plan—and even holding drills to test the plan— helps dispel the most persistent notions among some business people: If you ignore it, it will go away.

There are only two ways to handle a crisis: do something fast or ignore it. If you act immediately with openness, candor, and accessibility, chances are the crisis will end almost as fast as it starts. On the other hand, if you operate on the assumption that the crisis is none of anyone's business and you don't feel compelled to reveal anything, unless forced by circumstances or law, you will get burned.

Let's take two cases in 2005 involving President Bush. When Cindy Sheehan, the Gold Star mother who lost her son in the Iraq fighting, first went to Crawford, Texas, where President Bush was vacationing, she wanted the president to come out and talk to her. He should have talked to her for a couple of minutes within the first one or two days of her arrival. Two top administration officials had talked to Sheehan but the president never did.

Sure, he had met with her months earlier when she was in a group of other mothers who lost sons or daughters in Iraq. But at that point, when Bush was on vacation, Sheehan was accompanied by only a handful of supporters. It would have been easy to meet with her again. The president could have answered her question one more time about why her son, Casey, died in Iraq, and again, express his condolences. She had no following at the time and was just a lone, grieving mother. Sheehan would have gotten her 15 minutes of fame and slipped into oblivion.

Instead, someone gave President Bush the wrong advice, or he just acted on his own bad judgment, ignorant of crisis communications. As President Truman used to say, "The buck stops here."

Once the Sheehan protest started growing, it was too late. If President Bush had met Sheehan after the crowds and controversy started growing, he would have been acting under threat and doing so would have been wrong.

As a result, Sheehan soon became what the *New York Times* called, "a news media phenomenon" and a strong leader in the anti-Iraq War movement. Google, the Internet search engine, reported well over 5 million linked mentions of Cindy Sheehan. Even she admitted she was grateful President Bush did not meet with her. "If he'd met with me, then I would have gone home, and it would have ended there," she told the press.

While still on vacation weeks later, President Bush almost got it right. The president cut short his month-long vacation and returned to Washington to meet with his cabinet, former Presidents Bush and Clinton, and the task force established to coordinate the efforts of 14 federal agencies involved in the Hurricane Katrina disaster. Actually, he was a day late from traveling to the Gulf states. The one-day delay hurt the president because the media expected him to be on the scene as quickly as he was right after the terrorist attacks on the World Trade Center. In a crisis situation, you must act immediately.

Kevin McCauley, editor at O'Dwyer's newsletter, summed up the majority thinking of President Bush's one-day delay in a column posted on the O'Dwyer Web site in September 2005:

> President Bush has made a sweet recovery from the initial bungling of Hurricane Katrina. One prays that Bush is sincere in his effort. New Orleans isn't a quick-fix. The President needs to commit the remainder of his term to rebuilding one of America's greatest cities. One fears that Bush is playing a PR game, scouting for "Mission Accomplished" photo-ops. For instance, Bush's Sept. 15 nationally televised speech from Jackson Square outlining recovery plans probably brought a tear to the eye of President Reagan's handler Mike Deaver.
>
> The White House advance team hauled in floodlights and generators to the blacked-out area, framing the magnificent St. Louis Cathedral behind the President's podium. The lights brought joy to the few people braving the curfewed streets, blogged NBC anchorman Brian Williams.
>
> The area was lit about a half hour before the Presidential motorcade arrived. The lights went out an hour after Bush concluded his speech, plunging the streets into complete darkness. It is a PR stunt like the Jackson Square episode that makes one wonder about the Bush Administration's heart to the City of New Orleans.

The president eventually turned things around with frequent trips to New Orleans and visits with the city's mayor.

In the private sector, Wal-Mart got it right during Hurricane Katrina. They decided quickly to give aid to Gulf Coast victims. Of course, it also helped their badly tattered image at the time. The company gave $17 million in cash to the Clinton-Bush Katrina Fund, the American Red Cross, and the Salvation Army. They gave another $3 million in goods to shelters set up to house victims of Katrina, and established mini-Wal-Marts in the area to dispense clothing, diapers, food, and water free of charge.

THE WAL-MART PR MACHINE

O'Dwyer's McCauley called Wal-Mart CEO Lee Scott's Astrodome tour with Presidents Bush (the elder) and Clinton a "priceless photo-op." Wal-Mart hired the Edelman PR firm to promote its Katrina relief efforts.

Sharon Weber, Communications Manager for Wal-Mart, told me the O'Dwyer column "gives too much credit to Edelman for the success of our recovery effort."

"Our associates (PR staffers) deserve the credit for taking care of their communities and customers as they do every day. Edelman helped us share the success to the inquiring media; but it was the associates who did the work."

Weber said the Wal-Mart in-house PR department consists of 16 associates. Some of their crisis PR planning resulted in the creation of a war room inside the headquarters of Wal-Mart headquarters in Bentonville, Arkansas. Adopting the tactics of political campaigns, their rapid response team included former presidential advisors to Presidents Reagan and Clinton.

Colburn Aker, managing partner of the Aker Partners PR firm in Washington, D.C., said Hurricane Katrina made one thing "strikingly clear: Communications must be a top priority during times of crisis."

He offered the following tips derived from his agency's experience in working with the media in the hours and weeks following a crisis:

- Establish yourself as a credible news source from the first day.
- Provide frequent updates—avoid long gaps between contacts.
- Be prepared to answer hard questions.
- If an issue is outside your expertise, say so.
- Be available to take calls and interviews 24/7, and note the news doesn't stop on the weekends. Reach out to weekend media.

CRISIS AT HOME

Having the eye of Hurricane Wilma over my home in Palm Beach County, Florida, gave me a good vantage point to see how crisis communications works.

The Florida Power & Light company (FPL), instead of being overly optimistic, promised resumption of service in about a month. When power returned to my neighborhood after six days, I was elated. By giving a worst-case scenario, the company scared people up front, leaving them dreading weeks without electricity, but pleased if power returned sooner.

In a front-page business-section article in the *South Florida Sun-Sentinel* titled "Storms pose PR crisis for utilities," Jeff Zbar wrote:

> Crisis communications is a public relations field unto itself. Marketing departments conduct drills and train on how to respond to a crisis. The rapid-fire spread of news and rumors by Internet and worldwide news services has forced the

need for immediate reaction to curtail bad publicity whether from an accident, product malfunction or corporate malfeasance. The objective: Manage the release of information well to limit damage to your image.

Bad timing can be another problem after a disaster, as FPL learned. Two weeks after Hurricane Wilma, FPL went before the Public Service Commission to request an increase in its fuel adjustment charges. I doubt they consulted with their PR department before making that announcement.

Zbar quoted me several times in his article, including my statement, "(Utility) companies have to explain their outages and do it fast."

To see crisis communications work at its best, look at the airline industry. When a plane crashes, the airline PR people do everything in their power to get as much information to the press, particularly passenger names, so the story doesn't hang around longer than it should.

The best corporate handling of a crisis I have ever heard was Johnson's & Johnson's handling of a 1982 case of cyanide poisoning of its Tylenol product. The company pulled products from store shelves until tamper-resistant packaging had been implemented. Company CEO James Burke was open to the media and clearly presented management's commitment to fighting for the company's rights and its reputation.

Sometimes PR practitioners have to stop an action that they believe may cause bad publicity and a crisis. During the 1970s gasoline shortage, my boss, U.S. Senator Jim Buckley, told me he was going to Saudi Arabia to meet with King Faisal. He was scheduled to travel with an attorney representing Con Edison, New York's utility provider, who wanted to build a refinery. I thought it wouldn't look good and told the senator that helping a utility company and a lawyer could backfire. No argument. He cancelled the trip.

PR-PITS

Some people, like the folks at Wal-Mart, are PR-perfect. Some are PR-pits—they are the pits as far as public relations instincts or mastery are concerned. High up on my top ten of all-time PR-pits award winners is the U.S. Postal Service's public relations office for the southeastern section of the country, working out of the Atlanta office.

At the time of the 9-11 terrorist attacks of the World Trade Center, I was an investigative reporter and columnist for a chain of weekly newspapers in Palm Beach County, Florida. One week after the attacks, there was a bomb scare and three weeks later anthrax was discovered in my local post office. This was the facility that forwarded the anthrax letter(s) a few miles to the south to the AMI building in Boca Raton, which housed the *National Enquirer* and other tabloid publications. Ultimately one death to an *Enquirer* photo editor was blamed on the anthrax letter.

Weeks later, two whistleblowers from the post office contacted me. They charged management failed to decontaminate the post office of anthrax. They were worried for their lives. I called the local postmaster for comment. He refused to talk to me. I wrote two articles and then received a telephone call from some PR person who called the stories "a piece of crap," among other things. My third story, containing those comments, was even bigger than the first. Had no one called, or someone with some PR savvy called, I probably never would have written anything else about the post office after my first two pieces.

An amazing sidebar to the bomb scare and sidebar story happened in January 2006. The USPS responded to the newspaper's Freedom of Information request more than four years later.

As it turned out, I wrote some 60 articles about horrible conditions in post offices around the country over a two-year period. The articles were posted on a well-read post office watchdog Web site on the Internet, *www.postalwatch.net.* I was called a hero to postal workers. The series developed into a *cause celebre* for postal workers throughout the country. Never once did anyone from the Atlanta office follow up, nor did their superiors in Washington.

In another situation, in April 2006, I wrote an exclusive article for the *Lake Worth Herald* quoting a source saying that the city's electrical department purchased parts allegedly damaged by Hurricane Wilma.

No official of the city immediately commented on the article. Finally, after six days, the mayor called the *Herald* report "irresponsible." Of course, the mayor's charge was reported in a story under a banner headline.

The mayor and officials failed twice in this crisis situation. First, they should have responded to the newspaper immediately after my story was published. Next, they should have laid out the facts and not engaged in name calling with the media.

The city kept the story alive when I came up with additional facts in a third article.

RULES FOR DEVELOPING A CRISIS PLAN

In general, crisis response programs feature three phases: identify the problem, develop the solution, and communicate the action to all of the publics. When you are in the middle of a fast-breaking emergency, you may have to do all these things almost simultaneously and under tremendous pressure. That is why it is vital to have a specific, detailed plan, and to make sure everybody knows how to work the plan. Here are some steps for handling the basics of crisis management:

1. Draw up a comprehensive crisis action plan.
2. Isolate a crisis team from daily business concerns to focus on the problem. Centralize and control the flow of infor-

mation through the crisis team. Only designated and well-prepared people should talk to the media. Train spokespersons in advance on the company's posture and its message strategy.

3. Develop a strategy based on a worst-case scenario. Think of the worst things that could happen, then gear your strategy to those eventualities.

4. Aim at containment, not suppression. Local crises may become national and even international problems because of a failure to handle communications effectively at the local level. Put the problem into proper perspective for the media. Try to contain it geographically or to one kind of incident.

5. Know potential allies in advance and call on them. Identify public and private groups whose interests may overlap yours in a time of crisis. Line up third-party support.

6. While most crises, even if severe, break fast and are over fast, have a long-term crisis plan ready.

7. Rehearse the crisis team. Hold periodic workouts. Occasionally test the system with a "fire drill."

If the city government of New Orleans and the state government of Louisiana had crisis plans in place and followed them after Hurricane Katrina, the outcome most assuredly would have turned out better.

Scapegoating is a common reaction in a time of trouble. Businesspeople facing a crisis naturally ask, "Who's responsible for this?" The search for a culprit is a high-priority item—*if* it will help end the crisis more quickly, or if the company is being blamed for something that can be proved to be somebody else's responsibility. If either of these conditions exists, it's best not to make the assessment of blame one of the early goals. Be quick with the facts, slow with the blame.

TRY A MOCK CRISIS

Remember fire drills in school? They also work in crisis communication. Let's take a look at how a drill works. Porsche Cars North America (PCNA), located in Reno, Nevada, was once my client. I knew zero about what goes on under the hood of a car, but I knew the secrets of crisis management. At Porter Novelli, we had developed a crisis action plan for Porsche. Now, we were going to test Porsche on its understanding of how the company would handle itself in a crisis. We agreed we would do a drill. Callers would announce they were participating in Project Ambush and then they would take the role of a reporter or another participant. Key people at Porsche knew a drill was coming within a specified window of time, but they did not know any of the details or how it would unfold. Porsche was in the middle of a major advertising blitz featuring the high-performance aspects of their cars. One night, Porsche had a two-minute commercial scheduled to run during *Monday Night Football* on ABC. One week after that, Porsche was to open a vital Dealer Council Meeting in Los Angeles.

At 8:05 AM, one of my staffers, posing as a newspaper reporter, called PCNA headquarters asking for a comment regarding an accident that had just happened on a winding mountain road involving a Porsche sports car and a school bus carrying 40 children. The preliminary police report stated that the car had been going at speeds in excess of 90 miles per hour. For several hours, calls from other "reporters" poured in. The questions were getting increasingly sharp and difficult. Did Porsche stand behind the driver? Had the driver been on a training run for an upcoming race? Why was he driving 90 miles per hour? What would Porsche say to the parents of the dead and injured children? When would company officials meet with the media and answer questions?

We continued the calls posing as reporters, as well as consumer advocates, Porsche car dealers, and Ted Koppel, who asked for someone from Porsche to come on his *Nightline* television program to speak on the topic of driving safety. The chairman of a key congressional committee told Porsche the committee was considering the possibility of holding hearings.

The Project Ambush team from Porter Novelli monitored the entire exercise, which ran from 8:00 AM to 1:00 PM. The agency team was ready to respond to whatever decisions the Porsche crisis team made. For example, Porsche decided to hold a press conference, and agency people were ready in Reno to act as the media, firing the toughest questions and showing maximum skepticism at the answers.

Following Project Ambush, there were thorough debriefing sessions, discussions, and critiques, with extensive input from Porsche people. The end result for Porsche was some revision of the crisis plan. Probably the biggest benefit was Porsche's key personnel got their baptism under fire on how to handle a major emergency, and they emerged better prepared to handle the real thing. CEO Brian Bowler said he had never been under as much stress in his life as he was during the drill that he knew in advance was not the real thing. All in all, Porsche did well because they had a plan to follow.

MARTHA STEWART

The Martha Stewart story is a classic public relations case study. Stewart was sentenced in 2004 to five months behind bars and five months of house arrest after she was convicted of lying to authorities about her 2001 sale of about 4,000 shares of stock. She is on probation until March 2007 during which time she is not allowed to get drunk, own a gun, or leave the federal court district without permission . . . or practice bad public relations.

Fraser Seitel wrote in O'Dwyer's newsletter:

Martha was a moron to trust that her lawyers knew best about how to handle the public relations crisis swirling around her. She should have voluntarily admitted her mistake publicly and pleaded for "mercy and understanding" in the court of public opinion.

She didn't and was sent to the slammer.

Seitel believes Stewart learned during her jail time. One reason she is back, Seitel wrote, is

[she] shed the shyster attorneys who counseled her into the mess in the first place and started listening to common sense public relations advice.

Where her former PR strategies—cryptic public statements, hiding behind lawyers, a self-righteous Web site for her fans, etc., were insipid, her current PR strategy is inspired.

She has decided no longer to hide and to begin to control her own agenda, rather than letting others control it for her.

OPRAH MIFFED

Hermes, the upscale French clothing store, learned the hard way they should read up on crisis communications. In the fall of 2005, Hermes's flagship store in Paris turned away Oprah Winfrey, one of the wealthiest and most famous women in the United States. Oprah was mad at the rudeness of a Hermes employee. When the incident hit the American press, Hermes released a statement that Oprah implied that "[she] was some *diva* trying to get in when the stores was closed," according to the *New York Times*. More bad publicity; something the French get plenty of.

NEXT TIME

In summary, the essence of handling emergencies, for the short and long term, is to have a workable plan and to drill key people on implementing that plan if disaster strikes. The plan must have an authoritative spokesperson, openness and truthfulness with the media, and a quick response to the unpredictable twists and turns of the situation. It usually doesn't cost money to follow this thinking.

Good luck on your next crisis. There will be a next crises, just as sure as there will be another hurricane, homicide, terrorist attack, raging fire, or other horrific happening.

14

INTERNET PUBLIC RELATIONS
The New PR

Not a day goes by when I don't marvel over the Internet. Often times, I ask myself what I did before this phenomenon came along. I found out the hard way one week in October 2005 when the eye of Hurricane Wilma blew over my home office and left me without power for one week. When my power did come on, I was like a kid on Christmas morning as I watched my computer booting up after seven days in the dark.

In my early days in PR, the communications business was simple. There were three major television networks in the United States and no Internet. Today, in the United States there are more than 100 cable stations, 18,000 magazines, 300 million Web pages, and over 2 million Web sites.

PR veteran Al Golin, whose Golin-Harris firm is more than 50 years old, points out the opportunities today: "Anyone with an Internet connection and a point of view can potentially influence public opinion. Times have truly changed, but the need to communicate has not."

Yes, the Internet has arrived in a big way. You better get with it or get out of PR! What's good about the Interent is the small practitioner has the same opportunities for success in public relations as the giant companies.

Never in our lifetime has news been produced and spread as fast as it is today online. That's good and bad. With Internet PR you must be doubly careful of the facts; a mistake may be distributed worldwide.

However, with the Web you can correct mistakes instantly and get it out to the masses. In print, mistakes are harder to correct. An article with wrong facts may take up a quarter of a page and a correction of a sentence or two is run in a correction column, and usually not read by most people.

We all receive fraudulent e-mail. Often, it's about a political subject or someone spreading a false rumor. I once received a transcript of what purported to be an Andy Rooney *60 Minutes* broadcast. Most people would have accepted the words and thoughts to be that of the TV curmudgeon. I was skeptical. I typed in *www.snopes.com,* a Web site that tells you whether something that is getting widespread distribution is fact or fiction. I was right. The alleged Rooney broadcast was a fraud.

Veteran PR practitioner Bob Stone, a partner in the Dilenschneider Group, says that PR people today who do not think way outside of the box cannot know how to use the Internet as though it was their own printing press.

Stone told me:

> For example, I didn't realize until I started researching that CBS Radio Online News Service broadcasts two-minute Business News features and those who are not aware of this, are missing an opportunity.
>
> We all remember when marketing and advertising looked at us as their "toys." We sure did a good job of letting people know that we were not part of marketing and advertising, and

that we did not have to pay to get a client's name in the paper. Because of the great opportunities available today on the Internet, advertising and marketing agencies welcome PR ideas. In fact, it is amazing how many advertising and marketing campaigns on the Internet today are built around PR. There will always be a need in the corporate and financial world for strong and experienced public relations counsel. If this professional understands the Internet and knows what it can do, he will become the ultimate professional.

Today, the serious PR professional has at his/her fingertips more opportunities than we ever had years ago because of the Internet. Those at the beginning of a career in communication today, have opportunities we never dreamed of: A whole new way of getting worldwide publicity without having to call a press conference.

WORDS FROM A GEEK

I'm not a "geek" (an expert in a technical field, particularly with computers) so I went looking for some of the best minds to get their thoughts about the Internet and public relations.

Ed Schipul is more than a geek. He started his Houston-based company, Schipul—The Web Marketing Company, in 1997. He has strong opinions about the relationship between the Internet and public relations.

Schipul told me he sees the Web as the epicenter of interpersonal and organizational communications, giving the strategic public relations practitioner the ability to disseminate and receive information with more immediacy, flexibility, and cost effectiveness.

Schipul's firm helps its international client base integrate the latest Web technologies into their public relations and marketing efforts. Their proprietary Tendenci software serves as the backbone of numerous organization Web sites, including the

Houston and Memphis chapters of the Public Relations Society of America.

Tendenci makes blogging, podcasting, reader ratings, online surveys, online calendars, event registration, directories, and e-newsletters easy, says Schipul.

SEARCH ENGINES AND PUBLIC RELATIONS

Google, Yahoo, MSN.com, and other Internet search engines serve as the ultimate third-party endorsement of an organization. Web users know intuitively that a high ranking in the search engines means an organization's site offers the information they are seeking and is a respected site. In addition, search engines can account for a very significant portion of a company's online revenue, by providing links back to a Web site. That's why Schipul believes the responsibility for search engine optimization should be a public relations function. He notes:

The strategic public relations practitioner generally is responsible for establishing and strengthening relationships with trusted independent entities in order to encourage implicit or explicit endorsements. Historically, journalists have been the focus of PR's strategies, but we believe that search engines deserve the same level of respect and attention.

How do search engines work? They rely on an amazingly complex system that uses search engine spiders to constantly sweep the Internet and catalogue its contents. The methods of identifying and ranking Web pages are constantly changing; however, search engines evaluate three primary criteria:

1. *The Web site's navigation.* If a search engine spider can't get to a page because of a broken link or it is off limits without

a password, the page doesn't stand a chance of being ranked. Like your Web users, search engines don't like flash intros, so insist on simple navigation with a minimum number of clicks to get to any information. Having a site map is also important.

2. *The density of keywords on a page.* Ever notice how politicians always seem to say the same thing over and over? While a public relations writer may be tempted to use synonyms in order to make copy seem less repetitive, this actually undermines their efforts to get a message across. Political strategists understand this and so do search engines, which reward sites for disciplined message delivery by evaluating the relative density of keywords and phrases on a Web page.

3. *The number of relevant sites that link to your page.* If other individuals and organizations have determined that your page is worth linking to, the search engines pay attention. But don't fall for nefarious link-trading schemes. The search engines evaluate the quality as well as the quantity of links and can penalize a site that appears to be cheating.

Schipul encourages public relations practitioners to incorporate the concepts of maximizing keyword density and encouraging relevant link backs into their PR strategies. This way, every news release, e-newsletter, and speech can be accessed by those who are thirsty for that information at that moment.

For instance, when issuing a news release, consider the words and phrases that might be used to search for the information you are presenting. This can be challenging for public relations pros who sometimes can be a little flamboyant with their language.

An example is the manufacturer who announced a new line of high-end sinks. When crafting their news release, they didn't think the word *sink* had enough panache, so they substituted *water basin*.

To the online world, the news release was essentially invisible because nobody was searching for *water basin.*

This is the trouble with thinking like a company advocate instead of thinking like your customers. Their customers were in the market for a sink. When they went online, they typed *sink* into the search engines.

When writing news releases, e-newsletters, white papers, and other materials, always think like your target public and use the same words and phrases they would use.

"Search engines help remove the gatekeepers that used to stand between the public relations pro and the people they wanted to reach," said Schipul. "Now, when someone is seeking information on any particular subject, they typically use a search engine and link directly to the source of the information—rather than a journalist's interpretation of that information."

EMERGING SOCIAL TECHNOLOGIES AND PUBLIC RELATIONS

In the years since the introduction of the first Web browser, the Internet has been considered an interactive communications tool, but we're just beginning to scratch the surface in terms of unlocking the Web's ability to help us truly interact. Instead, organizations have reverted to old habits and have used the Web primarily to disseminate information.

Many company Web sites mimic corporate brochures. Even though the Web makes frequent updates possible, most corporate sites remain static for long periods. Most company Web sites still take a sequential approach to presenting their information: First we'll tell you this, and then click here and we'll give you that.

That may have been a powerful use of the Web in 1995, but it's completely outdated today. Search engines have turned the Web into an enormous user-driven and nonlinear repository of information. Instead of the information source dictating how information is presented and consumed, the user is in charge.

MY DAUGHTER AND MARRIOTT

My daughter, Michelle Saffir, is a manager for online products at Marriott International.

"What I can tell you is that on *Marriott.com*, the company had $2.7 billion gross revenues in 2005," Michelle told me.

Michelle stresses the importance of personalization to respond to individual needs of each customer and to tailor applications and contents based on the user:

> It is up to us to figure out what should change in the space the user perceives. Some sites remember who you are—as simple as a friendly greeting with your name—what your interests are, and provide content and links that are just for you.

Link personalization is widely used at *www.amazon.com* to link recommendations for you based on your previous site activity. As Michelle indicates:

> Users are more likely to respond to messaging if it is somehow applicable to the task they are performing and does not take users off their main course of action. In this way, it is generally viewed as a value-add for them and a way to build relationships.
>
> But while personalization can greatly improve sales, the primary focus should always be on mastering the basics first like usability and ease of navigation. In addition the customized information has to be presented in such a way that it doesn't preclude other information that may also be of value to the customer.

In mid-2006, the Marriott site was receiving more than 13 million visits a month with visitors spending 1.6 million hours on the site. This is six times more than the voice channels, according to Michelle.

When *Marriott.com* was launched in 1996, one reservation was made per hour. In 2006, the site generated approximately 1,400 reservations per hour.

If Web users don't find what they are looking for quickly—studies have shown that it may only take a few seconds—they click away. They may even take a negative impression of your brand with them.

This evolution of the Web as a dynamic, user-driven medium is something public relations practitioners have generally failed to grasp, let along capitalize upon. The desire to be in control of message delivery has muffled their willingness to participate in an incredible social experiment.

PR: BEHIND THE CURVES

Ed Schipul believes:

Public relations people typically want to control all aspects of their communications programs to the smallest detail, but the true power of the Web only comes when you relinquish some of that control. By giving Web users the ability to add and edit Web content, you can foster a community and build an indelible connection between the users and your brand.

As the pace of change accelerates, other user-driven technologies are becoming standard on the Web. Many of these tools have not been embraced by the public relations community, even though they lend themselves to powerful PR applications.

Social Web-based technologies were initially referred to as consumer-generated media, but this label proved to be too restrictive for the sea change that has been occurring. As a result, the in crowd is referring to the rise of social Web-based technologies as Web 2.0. This accurately reflects that the Web is no longer a collection of discreet Web sites. Instead, it is a platform for information sharing. Schipul states:

> We are now in a world where everyone has a voice and where everyone is part of the conversation. Generally, PR strategists are behind the curve in terms of understanding how to leverage these technologies to achieve greater results through improved flexibility and cost efficiencies. They want to keep it business as usual even though a revolution is occurring.

The Internet is so dynamic that specific examples are likely to be outdated even before this book is printed. But here are a few examples that are likely to last.

Communities

Craigslist.org is a great example of a Web site that got the word out, built a community, and created a phenomenon that took off and is now known all over. It is one of the most popular sites in the world. It was started by Craig Newmark in 1995 to tell people about cool events in the San Francisco area. It spread by word of mouth and has cut into the newspaper business by siphoning off their advertising dollars in classifieds such as job listings, items for sale, and apartment listings. More than 6 million classified ads and 1 million forums are posted every month. It gets about 3 billion page views per month and more than 10 million people use it each month. Craigslist's largest category is New York Apartments, where it posts more than half a million listings a month, according to an article in *New York Magazine* in January 2006.

Blogs

The term *blog* is short for Weblog and initially referred to on-line diaries. Because most blogs offer readers the opportunity to post comments, they provide an opportunity for two-way communication that implicitly tells Web users their input is valued.

Blogs quickly gave rise to the concept of consumer-generated media—the idea that journalism was no longer only for professionals at newspapers or broadcast outlets. For better or worse, through blogs, virtually anyone can be a journalist or commentator. And, like professional journalists, if their information is interesting, entertaining, or otherwise valuable, they can attract an audience.

Shipul asked me to answer a PR question for him in a blog he operates. I did, and within a day, I received a Google Alert with my blogged item.

How powerful are blogs? One of the most stunning aspects of the 2004 presidential election was the investigative reporting by bloggers to undermine a *60 Minutes* exposé on President Bush's service in the National Guard. It led to the retirement of Dan Rather, one of the most powerful television journalists in the world.

From a public relations perspective, the rise in influence of some blogs presents unique challenges. Like traditional media outlets, getting positive coverage in a blog can help build awareness of, and demand for, your brand among a highly desirable audience. But be careful; there are no rules in the blogosphere. Commit a PR blunder and you could be publicly chastised.

The best advice is to become familiar with a target blog and only approach bloggers with information that they would find valuable.

Alternatively, some public relations pros are now operating blogs on behalf of their companies or clients to keep customers and prospects up to date on industry news, trends, tips, and special offers. If you are considering starting a blog for your organization, firm, or business, keep in mind that blog comments are written in a conversational style, which tells your visitors that you respect them and you are ready to join in a conversation on their terms.

Many organizations that publish a newsletter now include much of that same content in their blog. Why wait to package all that valuable information in newsletter form? Make valuable information available as soon as you have it!

Some PR pros have even used blogs to extend the reach of their fictional characters. For instance, the Jack-in-the-Box fast food chain caused a stir by giving Jack his own blog; and one of the characters in the sitcom *How I Met Your Mother* not only has a blog but mentions it occasionally on the show.

One other benefit of having a blog on your corporate Web site is that it can help improve a Web site's search engine performance. This is particularly true if the content is relevant to your users and includes the keywords and phrases prospects are searching for.

Really Simple Syndication

Usually shortened to RSS, this is a tool that has gained momentum as a result of the overwhelming volume of new content hitting Web sites every day. Basically, RSS helps Web users track new Web content that is of interest to them without searching for it. Instead, links to news, articles, and Web site updates they care about are delivered to them via a feed reader. This RSS feed reader searches user-specified RSS-enabled Web sites on the Internet and sends updates directly to the user's computer.

By giving Web users the ability to subscribe to receive up-dates, RSS rewards public relations practitioners for providing great Web content. The more valuable your information is to your target audience, the more likely they'll be to subscribe to receive your RSS feed.

One of the reasons that RSS has been compared favorably to the use of e-mail is that it is completely opt-in with no possibility of forcing someone to read an RSS feed.

The *Bulldog Reporter's* Media Relations Insider reports the fol-lowing:

> In the modern communications world, it's now clear that the blogosphere is the place to be. PR pros can now quickly and easily access news about trend activity and competitors' announcements, as well as monitor public perception of their companies and products online. RSS feeds make it easier to customize and organize information for your audiences.

Wikis

The incredible popularity of Wikipedia, the online encyclope-dia that is completely generated by Web users, has prompted some public relations pros to explore how to harness the power of com-munity building and collaboration.

A wiki is a Web application that allows users to add content, as on an Internet forum. It also allows anyone to edit the content.

Using wikis, the PR community can now collaboratively pro-duce how-to guides and tips and tricks associated with their offer-ings. In fact, your customer community will generate these whether you are ready or not. A great example is the wealth of knowledge sharing taking place in the online gaming community, with gam-ers explaining shortcuts that help each other unlock hidden fea-tures in video games.

Rather than resist, adventurous PR folks are joining in the conversation by using Wiki-based online collaboration to help with message development and even product design.

At a minimum, wikis enable greater collaboration within the PR department. Why e-mail a document back and forth when you can collaborate on it in real time?

Tagging

At its core, this is a keyword-filing system in which the consumers of the content—and not just the originator—participate in how the content is categorized. Tagging acknowledges that each of us has a unique point of view and that the same information may have very different meaning to different people.

Both the author and Web users assign tags by what makes sense to them; more popular content is displayed more prominently based on user interaction and feedback.

Ultimately, by tagging, everyone is contributing to a shared set of resources filed under that tag. What results is a community-built categorization system that reflects how individuals describe the content on your site, rather than a highly structured location system. It can transform a company's Web site into a dynamic user-driven information source.

From a public relations perspective, tagging is an opportunity to listen to the market. It represents dynamic real-time research! It tells us at that moment how Web users prioritize our information and how they describe it. What can be more insightful than that? Search engine keyword counts and popular tags are windows into understanding the customer's perspective, which can help us better serve end users with high-value offerings.

Podcasts and Vlogs

The popularity of iPods has contributed to the rise of audio podcasts and video podcasts, also called vlogs. Similar to blogs, podcasts and vlogs are typically created by individuals on subjects of niche interest. They are disseminated through individual Web sites, RSS feeds, and software such as Apple's iTunes.

Anyone with a computer and a recording device can publish a podcast or a vlog. Even modestly equipped cell phones can be used to record and download audio and video, which is contributing to the rise of consumer-generated media.

By recognizing that presenting information through pictures, sound, and compelling stories is a superior way of educating, engaging, and mobilizing audiences, public relations pros can use podcasts and vlogs to reach highly targeted niche audiences.

For instance, by producing podcasts that discuss relevant topics for its target audience, an organization can strengthen its positioning as an industry leader and provide an opportunity to describe the related products and services being offered. The creative possibilities are endless.

And internally, podcasts and vlogs can also be used to build awareness of company initiatives. No need to call everyone to the conference room to watch a corporate video about the latest safety program or change to company benefits. A podcast or vlog can achieve the same goal more efficiently while also providing an immediate feedback mechanism to help clarify points.

Like search engines, Web 2.0 technologies further enable Web users to control their online experience. The term Web 2.0 refers to a second generation of services available on the Web that lets people collaborate and share information online. By enabling the user to add and edit content, these technologies go a giant step further. And, for the first time ever, PR professionals have the ability to easily and cost-effectively interact directly with their publics on a large scale. By implementing these Web technologies, public relations pros can employ powerful new strategies to reach and influence their targets.

Eric Schwartzman, managing director of Schwartzman & Associates, a boutique public relations firm based in Los Angeles, warns that podcasts are heard by a very motivated, tech-savvy audience of early adopters and as such should not be underestimated. Schwartzman told me:

> Don't be afraid to experiment. Just as stage productions iron out the kinks during previews, don't be afraid to change and adapt your podcast over time. The rules are still emerging so don't be afraid to let your audience help you refine your concept by soliciting feedback.

TESTING

Jay Berkowitz, president of the online marketing firm Ten Golden Rules located in Boca Raton, Florida, told me the secret to success on the Internet is to "test, test, and retest":

> Testing is easy and inexpensive and like direct marketing, Internet marketing is very measurable. It is easy to measure the number of people who visit a Web site, where they came from and what they do when they get to the site. What keywords did they type in to Google or another search engine to find you? Which press releases generated the most site visits? Which photos get the most interest?

> Entire campaigns should be built based on measurements and analysis of real, factual data, not on hypotheses that can be wrong. In the end, I like what PR veteran Al Golin told me:

There is a problem, however, with a high-tech, low-touch culture. Many organizations are becoming increasingly reliant on impersonal communication. People are much more willing to use e-mail than to set up face-to-face meetings or even talk on the phone. This is part and parcel of the trend toward emotionless interactions that are starting to define business relationships. It is rare to witness the pitched, emotional battles that used to take place routinely not so many years ago. Back then, people used to argue, fight, and make up, and the relationships grew stronger over time.

Golin told me about a man who was in an office less than 30 feet from his who he regularly left voice-mail messages for, and he responded by calling back rather than by walking into his office and giving him his opinion.

I'm in love with the Internet and new technology, and I use it regularly. Go ahead and use IM (instant messaging) to your heart's content . . . as long as you still use the telephone or, even better, you still schedule meetings over a cup of coffee. I will never stop managing by walking around and picking up the telephone to call someone . . . and I will save much of my non-time-sensitive e-mailing for after-work hours.

15

PERFORMANCE-BASED AND LOW-BUDGET PR
Changing the Playing Field

John Elliott, founder and president of Power PR of Torrance, California, is changing the public relations playing field by guaranteeing story-placement success. Founded in 1991, Power PR is a marketing publicity firm that specializes in gaining publicity for consumer, industrial, and high-tech clients. Having enabled the publication of thousands of articles since its founding, the company's forte is generating a large number of published articles for its clients in campaigns designed to generate a large quantity of qualified leads.

Elliott brings over 37 years of public relations and marketing experience to the company. As a public relations executive, Elliott has been instrumental in landing hundreds of pages of print coverage and hundreds of hours of radio and television coverage for his various local, national, and international clients. He has secured press coverage for political, art, sports, telecommunications, manufacturing, medical, scientific, and many other organizations.

Elliott seldom goes with the flow. For the past seven years, he has led his publicity firm into a whole new realm of public relations; in fact, he has created a new category he calls "marketing publicity."

"Marketing publicity is a hybrid of marketing and PR that involves promoting a product or service through the mass media," Elliott told me. "By writing feature articles, customer testimonials, and new product releases and getting them placed in consumer or trade publications (online and print), a marketing publicity firm can generate many published articles over time to build brand awareness and generate a large quantity of qualified leads."

The power behind marketing publicity and conventional PR is its objective, third-party endorsement. First, these articles are often laden with positive customer testimonials. Second, the fact that the publication has published the article is also a form of third-party endorsement. Elliott says these factors add up to a level of credibility that is difficult to achieve with other business-to-business marketing techniques. Elliott contends that

> [the] ultimate goal of a business-to-business marketing publicity program is to drive in qualified leads that can be turned into sales. With an abundance of qualified leads, your sales increase, even if your margins are rather large. With enough sales, at hefty margins, your profits increase. When you expand consistently, month after month, you have money for things you need. You have money for people you need. Problems go away.

According to Elliott, marketing publicity will not only generate a volume of leads, it also improves the quality of leads. These leads are often superior because, after reading an article, prospects typically are more educated about a product on first contact with sales staff; view the information with much more credibility; and are more willing to accept the company as a legitimate player in the market. Elliott says

[m]arketing publicity can bring a product from nonexistence into national prominence in a matter of days. With this business-to-business marketing technique you can communicate to potentially millions of prospects at an extremely low overall cost per prospect. It can educate prospects about a complex product at a fraction of the cost of display advertising. It can establish credibility for a company and its products like no other marketing tool.

On behalf of its clients, Power PR utilizes the mass media, including trade publications, television, radio, newspapers, newsletters, and the Internet to communicate to every member of their prospect's decision-making team. When using marketing publicity, Elliott says

[r]esults such as 1,000 inquiries from a single article are not uncommon. We have had as many as 450 inquiries in one day, from one article. It is not unusual for a client to get 10 to 15 articles published in a month. We guarantee a client from 3 to 5 stories a month. With statistics like these we have no problem meeting that quota. Our clients clearly see there are real benefits to our marketing publicity over traditional "unsecured" PR.

GUARANTEED PUBLICITY

Elliott is not your typical PR man. He is mild mannered and soft spoken, yet he is the architect of one of the most significant methodological changes to affect the public relations industry in years—guaranteed-published stories, month-to-month contracts, and an unusual performance/statistics-driven program. His manufacturing and technology clients love it, and are getting more bang for their PR-buck than they have seen in a long time, if ever. Elliott says

> [j]ust as doctors have prospered for decades without ever guaranteeing a cure, the public relations profession has survived and thrived without guaranteeing any quantifiable results for their work. Now is the time for clients to demand measurable results. It will improve the performance and image of public relations in general. Once PR firms are judged by statistics, they will become truly accountable to their clients.

To this end, Power PR is the only marketing publicity firm I have found in the country that guarantees a specific number of published articles per month, insists on month-to-month contracts, and manages its clients by performance-based statistics. With Elliott's success, I am sure others will give it a try.

Elliott's call for accountability has riled some in the PR industry. Several have even argued that guaranteeing results is unethical, and cite paragraph 9 of the Public Relations Society of America's Code of Professional Standards: "A member shall not guarantee the achievement of specified results beyond the member's direct control."

According to Elliott, that makes no sense:

> Didn't Sears & Roebuck build its reputation by guaranteeing customer satisfaction? How could that be unethical? Don't thousands of reputable companies all over the country back up their products with guarantees? Wouldn't most people like to see *more* companies take greater responsibility for the success of their clients by guaranteeing specific results.

What might have prevented other PR firms from quantifying and guaranteeing their results was a mistaken belief that agencies have no control over the outcome of their work.

Some PR professionals even make clients feel uninformed if they expect or require specific results. If clients demand accountability, PR professionals may claim that clients do not understand PR. They tell clients that getting articles published is not like buying advertising. Public relations professionals have no control over editors, who decide what they will publish. PR professionals tell clients that there is a great deal of competition for space. All of these things are true, but they should not be used as excuses for lack of accountability or poor results, says Elliott.

NO LONG CONTRACTS

Besides guaranteeing clients three to five published articles per month, Power PR also offers its clients month-to-month contracts only. In other words, clients can quit at any time. The firm's most common program guarantees five published articles per month, beginning in month two. Monthly fees range from $4,000 to $7,000 per month on month-to-month contracts. Elliott said the following:

While I was setting up the program I noticed we generally did a better job with our month-to-month clients than with the annual-contract clients because we were always afraid we were going to lose them. So I established a new policy that Power PR would only offer month-to-month contracts. I felt that pressure would help us do a better job.

TRACKING ACTIVITIES

VPs of marketing, sales managers, CEOs, CFOs, and even COOs are waking up to the fiscal-driven reality that PR must justify its cost in much the same way that advertising does, according to Elliott. At Power PR, a number of marketing publicity activities can be tracked and analyzed to provide clients with objective criteria from which to measure the effectiveness of the PR effort.

At Power PR, seven basic parameters are monitored by Elliott's team. The PR firm tracks the first five, the client the last two.

1. Number of editors contacted
2. Number of editors considering a story
3. Number of articles scheduled for an upcoming issue (per week)
4. Number of published articles (per week)
5. Impressions per week (total published article circulation in relation to article size)
6. Article-generated responses
7. Cost per lead

Elliott claims

[n]ot knowing performance figures is like having a car without a speedometer—you don't know how fast or slow you're going. If you don't check your speed often enough, like weekly, then you could be down the road too far before you discover that you need to make a correction. Over time, these metrics provide valuable guidance. Each week should be compared to the next. By graphing the values over many weeks, trends can easily be noticed.

Over a period of two years, 2000 through 2001, Power PR surveyed 227 CEOs of $2 million to $50 million annual gross manufacturing companies. Of those, 81.2 percent said they were "unhappy" with their advertising results. This included display ads, direct mail, trade shows, telemarketing, card decks, and their respective Web sites. One CEO said the following:

In examining some of the ads placed by these manufacturing companies, we discovered that they were full of "product puffery" and unsubstantiated claims. In other words, most manufacturers surveyed used advertising to brag about themselves. Bragging has never been a very effective promotional strategy, especially when trust and credibility are not established first.

Elliott reports that prospective customers are suspicious of advertising. They tend not to believe unsubstantiated product claims. Your product may be better than your competition's product, but who is going to believe it if it is only you tooting your horn?

Elliott also states there is yet another problem with advertising called clutter. Clutter is defined as "a multitude of commercial messages delivered within a short period of time," according to *Webster's New World Dictionary of Media and Communications,* by Richard Weiner. Marketing expert Alexander Hiam, author of *Marketing for Dummies,* describes clutter this way:

> The average customer is exposed to thousands of marketing messages every day (including 1,500 ads alone, on average, through TV, radio, outdoor, and print media). The consumer fails even to notice most of them. Of the messages he or she notices, most are forgotten right away, and only a few manage to scratch the surface of consciousness. All these ads create a great deal of background noise.

While doing research on publicity years ago, advertising icon David Ogilvy discovered that six times more people read articles than ads. He also discovered that people believe what is written in articles. Consequently, he started designing and placing ads that looked like articles for his clients. This new type of ad generated many more leads than ads that looked like ads. In fact, this new form of advertising proved so effective that the government began requiring the word *advertisement* be placed at the top of such ads.

Today, Power PR writes legitimate news articles and feature stories, not advertisements. As such, they are not labeled as advertisements in publications. Editors are willing to publish submitted material—if it is appropriate and written in journalistic style—because it means one less article that they have to write themselves.

WHAT MAKES NEWS

Elliott's business model works like this. Editors have hundreds of articles to choose from so it's important to present your article in the best light. The first thing Elliott needs to know is the publication's purpose and the targeted readership. Then, when Elliott presents material to the editor, he explains how the story will help the editor achieve the publication's purpose. The story must also be written in tight, journalistic style. When these factors are present and the follow-up with the editor is consistent and effective, the story has a chance of being published.

To generate a large volume of published articles through the mass media, the client must have a product or service that is newsworthy. Power PR understands what makes news, and what doesn't. If a client has a product that is not newsworthy, Power PR can help the client make any necessary adjustments to make it newsworthy. This can often be done without changing the product at all.

Elliott described an example of this in the work his company did for American Motion Systems, who approached Elliott to promote a new type of electric motor they had invented. For strategic reasons, the owner of the company wanted a feature article about this new electric motor to appear in the *L.A. Times, San Francisco Examiner, Honolulu Advertiser,* and various other newspapers around the country where the investors in American Motion Systems were located. The owner wanted his investors to read about the product in their local morning newspaper while sitting at the breakfast table.

Although the news about this electric motor was newsworthy for the electric trade, it was not newsworthy for the popular press, including major local newspapers. Determined to find a solution, Elliott studied the technology carefully until he realized that it conformed to the engineering definition of an electric turbine. Elliott learned that there had been gas and steam turbines, but never in history had there been an electric turbine. This provided the angle he was looking for.

Once Elliott confirmed that he was correct, he asked American Motion Systems what major market would most benefit from the electric turbine. The automotive market was the answer. Elliott then contacted the Associated Press's automotive expert and told him about the first electric turbine in the history of the world, an invention that would be applicable to the automotive industry.

An article was subsequently published by the AP and distributed to member newspapers throughout the country, including the *San Francisco Examiner* and the *L.A. Times,* which ran a half-page article in the Sunday paper with multiple photos.

ALEX KONANYKHIN

When my second public relations book was in print and enjoying good sales in 2000, I thought I knew everything about PR and its future.

If someone had told me then that a 33-year-old Russian expatriate/former banker who was once a whiz-kid physics genius was going to challenge some of the giants in the PR industry in our country, I probably would have thought that person consumed too much vodka.

Russian Alex Konanykhin, who was granted political asylum by the United States in 1999, has, like Elliott, started taking on the PR giants by making it easier and cheaper to get ink.

Konanykhin is chief executive officer of KMGI, an online marketing and advertising agency he founded in 1997 that has offices in New York, Washington, D.C., and Toronto. His marketing tools and methodologies have been used by industry leaders including DuPont, Canon, GE, Volvo, and Pfizer.

Toward the end of 2005, he launched a subsidiary company called Publicity Guaranteed, based in Washington, D.C.

Unlike the traditional public relations service providers that charge fees whether or not media placement is achieved, Publicity Guaranteed only charges for actual placements secured on a client's behalf, and at rates well below the industry average.

Konanykhin has borrowed from Google's success.

"Google achieved enormous success by using a performance-based business model for online advertising, and we're now applying this proven methodology in the PR industry," Konanykhin told me.

Billing clients a relatively modest fee for only verified results is a completely new paradigm in public relations, according to Konanykhin. "Now for the first time, businesses large and small can reap the benefits and inherent value of publicity with no financial risk or uncertainty whatsoever."

Who knows, Hollywood may make a film about Konanykhin one of these days. His story has already been featured on CBS's *60 Minutes*. According to the *Wall Street Journal*, he was a pioneering Russian capitalist in the early 1990s after the fall of communism, who built a banking and investment empire valued at an estimated $300 million by his mid-20s. He was a member of Boris Yeltsin's inner circle. He blew the whistle on the KGB and its involvement in the banking industry and angered Russian leader Vladimir Putin. He fled Russia to the United States in 1992 and it took him years to convince an immigration judge that he should be given asylum.

After starting his ad agency, Konanykhin began selling software.

Konanykhin told me he believes that public relations will move more and more toward performance-based models just as the online advertising industry has done.

Publicity Guaranteed's rates range from $195 for newspapers with a circulation under 10,000 to $2,850 for major publications with circulations over 500,000, such as the *Wall Street Journal, USA Today,* the *New York Times,* the *Washington Post,* and the *Chicago Tribune.* Publicity Guaranteed says it doesn't do mass mail press releases but relies on targeted presentations to media contacts. The company writes the press releases for their clients. They claim they never fail to deliver less than ten placements.

In the first quarter of 2006, Konanykhin was promoting his company with large ads in the *New York Times.*

MARGIE FISHER

Konanykhin and John Elliott aren't the only two who practice performance-based pricing. Margie Fisher does as well. All three achieve a perfect 10 on the *PR on a Budget* scale.

Fisher started her own marketing and public relations business in 2001 in Boca Raton, Florida. With a degree in finance and a master's in business administration, Fisher had gained her experience working for traditional PR firms and Fortune 500 accounts. At first, she too operated within the traditional monthly fee model. But as time went on, she got valuable feedback from clients and prospects. Soon she learned the hard way that most small businesses didn't want to pay retainers of several thousand dollars a month without being assured of results. Fisher told me the following:

I often tell people that 99.9 percent of public relations firms today use the traditional public relations retainer model. That means they charge you a monthly fee with no promise of results of any kind. Retainer fees vary, from $3,000 to $10,000 a month, and higher, often with a minimum time commitment of 6 or 12 months. While this model works for many large firms, many small firms and organizations don't want to pay out that type of money without being assured of results.

Starting in January 2004, Fisher moved away from the traditional model and developed Do-It-Yourself Public Relations Workshops. "That was useful for many people, but there were others who didn't want to do their own PR," she told me. "They just wanted to have someone do it at a low cost." Businesspeople told Fisher they wanted a low-cost way to get media coverage. They were afraid they would pay a public relations firm thousands of dollars and they would get nothing in return.

After a great deal of research and tweaking, Fisher created the Pay-for-Results publicity program, where clients only pay if they get media coverage. Fees, paid only if she is successful, range from $500 to $6,000 depending on the medium.

"I love pitching and I have other team members who also love pitching. We don't do anything but media relations," Fisher says.

Fisher won't soon forget Steve Sims, her first Pay-for-Results client and the owner of Bluefish Concierge, a West Palm Beach–based transportation and entertainment company. Bluefish Concierge caters to executives, celebrities, and other well-heeled types who can afford to lease $250,000 automobiles and fly in Hollywood stars to perform at private parties. Margie hit jackpots with placements in a string of top-tier media including the *New York Times,* and the *Wall Street Journal* toward the end of 2005.

"I've worked with other public relations firms," says Sims, "but none competes with Margie. Her prices are better."

Beverly Rothstein, a real estate broker-associate with Exit Team Realty of Coral Springs, Florida, like her colleagues, knows a lot about advertising. She retained Fisher when she wanted to "take

[her] business to a higher level." In two months Rothstein received coverage in the *New York Times, Money Magazine,* the *Boston Globe, Toronto Star,* and the *Palm Bach Post.*

Pay-for-Results today represents about 80 percent of Margie Fisher's business.

Fisher says some clients wanted an even lower-cost public relations choice. Enter her Reduced Fee Publicity Program:

> The concept is simple. Let's say one of my staff is speaking with a reporter from *USA Today* and learns about a story the reporter is working on and she has a client who would be a good fit for it. That's where her reduced fee program kicks in. She is able to offer lower fees because she doesn't have to pitch the story idea, only the source, and this saves her a lot of time.

Fisher says she and her staff speak to many editors and reporters every day. "It just stands to reason that these journalists are seeking sources for other stories they're working on."

Wendy Almquist, owner of Boca Raton–based Beeswax Candle Company is one of Fisher's low-cost publicity clients. "Margie called and said the *Wall Street Journal* needed a source, and I fit the criteria. For a very small fee, my little company was featured in the nation's most prominent business publication."

Fisher's fees under the reduced-fee program are substantially lower than the pay-for-results program.

Along the way, Fisher, who hails from New Bedford, Massachusetts and is still under 40, learned the most important part of public relations: dealing with the media. Here's what Jeff Zbar, a highly respected journalist who writes for the *Sun-Sentinel* in south Florida and other regional and national media, has to say about Fisher:

> Margie's a pro. She responds quickly to my queries with appropriate leads, checks in to find out what I'm working on,

understands the nuance of the journalist-publicist relationship—and handles it all with skill and tact. I don't avoid her
calls—and as a working journalist, that's saying a lot.

In March of 2006, Fisher held a four-hour workshop called
"Pitch the Media for PR Coverage." She told do-it-yourselfers how
to develop story ideas, and gave them the opportunity of pitching
a panel of media made up of five south Florida–area reporters
and editors.

ANOTHER INNOVATIVE APPROACH

Also in Boca Raton, Tracy Tilson, recognizing the low-budget
market, added a new division to her traditional agency. Her firm,
Tilson Communications, which she started in 1989, handles full-
service PR for national clients such as Staples and BJ's Wholesale
Club. She has also introduced a new service to help small businesses
maximize their media coverage. Called PromptPR!, the service
offers an innovative approach to public relations that is easy to use
and affordable to new, small, and emerging businesses operating
within a tight budget. "With the influx of so many new entrepreneurs
into the business world—women starting their own businesses, all
of the new high tech and dot.com companies—PromptPR! is the
perfect tool to help them get the word out," Tilson told me.

She offers two different products.

Press Release Preparation

For $375, a new, small, or mid-sized business will receive

- a telephone consultation with an experienced PR professional
from Tilson Communications, who will research information

for a press release, including basic information about the business, the reason behind the press release, and the audience that the company wants to reach;

- a professionally written press release, utilizing proper journalistic style, provided to the client on disk, by e-mail, or as a paper master, ready for photocopying onto the company letterhead;

- a list of up to ten media contacts (both local and national trade), including reporters and assignment editors, specifically researched and selected for each individual client by Tilson Communications;

- current address labels for the ten recommended media contacts that the client can use for mailing the press release; and

- a copy of the fact-filled booklet *PR TIPS & TACTICS,* which contains suggestions for how to do an effective follow-up call to a reporter after the release has been sent, plus the appropriate etiquette for speaking with time-pressed reporters and editors.

Press Release Preparation and Media Distribution

For $550, a new, small, or mid-sized business will receive:

- the basic press release preparation product listed above, including the telephone consultation, the professionally written press release, and a copy of the *PR TIPS & TACTICS* booklet;

- distribution of the press release via Business Wire, the international media relations wire service, to all of the print and broadcast media outlets in the client's state, as well as to major news bureaus and publications such as AP,

Bloomberg, Dow Jones, Reuters, the *New York Times, USA Today*, and the *Wall Street Journal;*

- a list of up to 25 media contacts (both local and national trade), including reporters and assignment editors, specifically researched and selected for each individual client by Tilson Communications; and
- current address labels for the 25 recommended media contacts that the client can use for mailing the press release.

"By using PromptPR!, new, small, and mid-sized companies can have access to major-league PR expertise without an ongoing, budget-busting expense," Tilson added.

COMING SOON TO YOUR AREA

These four companies from across the country testify that if you don't want to do it yourself, there are others that will help you on a low budget.

Over the next five years, I predict more and more PR practitioners from the big agencies will open their own small businesses patterned like these examples. Maybe you are one of them. If so, e-mail the details to me *(Lenpr@bellsouth.net)* so I can add your company to the *PR on a Budget* story as I travel around the country talking to media.

16

THE WORTHY CAUSE
PR to the Rescue

Cause-related public relations is becoming a major element of PR. Large and small companies are tying the promotion of their goods and services to the promotion of causes of all kinds. This development is good for both the businesses and the causes.

Public funding has been severely curtailed. Private fundraising has gotten tougher as more causes battle for fewer dollars. When companies harness their PR power for worthy enterprises, both parties benefit. Companies believe that consumers will be more likely to support a company that supports a cause.

This form of public purpose is spreading all over the world, including Australia. The PR People, a public relations firm in Australia, calls cause-related marketing a "medium for motivating buyer behavior." They believe cause-related marketing is a more sophisticated approach than traditional areas of sponsorship.

In America, there are not necessarily more worthy causes now than there were before, but the causes are now well known. Poverty, drugs, disease, disasters—we face so many pressing problems, all in need of funding. And what about education? Scientific research? The arts? These goodwill causes, social issues, events, and situations are areas of opportunities for the small businessman or large corporation.

In the past, companies were very careful about becoming linked with causes. Nothing controversial was permitted. Depressing or downbeat themes were taboo. Companies did not want their names associated with anything ugly enough to conjure up bad thoughts. It was all right to be in favor of motherhood or against the man-eating shark, but it was deemed risky to become more adventurous than that.

PETER DRUCKER SAYS

Now, however, corporations are getting behind a wider variety of causes—relief for victims of hurricanes, tsunamis, floods, and earthquakes, plus every disease known to man. Take the subject of battered women and battered children. Domestic violence has been one of America's shameful secrets, kept in the closest for a long time. In the past, images conjured up by social violence were considered too unhappy and disturbing to associate with a product or company.

"What's in it for me" is beginning to change to "What can we do for you."

Companies that espouse causes cannot afford to ignore the potential for controversy. Companies should prepare for all the ways a cause might become controversial and should be ready to stick with the cause when controversy arises.

Should corporations contribute massively to charities? This has been a subject of debate among management philosophers like Peter Drucker, the political economist, author, and management consultant specializing in strategy and policy for businesses.

He has written more than 30 books, which have sold tens of millions of copies in more than 30 languages. Drucker maintains that managers of businesses must not damage the company's profit and survival chances by giving money away, but he also says, "Management has a self-interest in a healthy society, even though the cause of society's sickness is none of management's making." He staunchly defended the need for businesses to make money but always said that employees were a resource not a cost.

Drucker points out in his book *Managing for the Future* that the mission of nonprofits is their asset. Nonprofit organizations do not base their strategy on money, as many corporations do. Businesses start planning by discussing financial returns while nonprofits start with their performance of their mission, according to Drucker.

Tim Penning, a public relations consultant who heads up his own company called Penning Ink, says the following:

> There are obvious communications channels and publics common to non-profits and corporations. But the non-profit PR practitioner must think harder about whom to reach, and how. Non-profit organizations may struggle with smaller budgets and staffs for public relations activities. But non-profits do have an advantage in that most of them by nature have a clear and distinct mission.

Penning says that volunteers are a vital public that must be addressed by PR practitioners in nonprofits. They need to be reminded often of the mission, and their place in fulfilling it.

COMPANIES JUMPED IN

In 2005, when Hurricanes Katrina and Wilma hit Louisiana, Mississippi, Alabama, and Florida, and an earthquake struck Pakistan, scores of companies jumped in to help, and rightly so.

Cause-related, strategic public relations is a versatile tool. The cause can be big or small. A small business can generate great goodwill and interest in a community by skillfully supporting a cause. This means more than just buying an ad in the playbill of the community theater or furnishing uniforms to a Little League team. It means espousing a cause that sets a company apart from other companies; making skillful, restrained use of the PR opportunities presented; and sticking with the cause.

What could the bead store owner do? How about inviting customers in for lessons on how to make a necklace or a braclet. The finished products could be sold with all proceeds going to a local charity. Local newspapers, radio, and television would do an item on this.

Sticking with the cause is vital. An association with a cause rarely produces a big sales bonanza right off the bat. This is a good reason why an association with a cause is better handled by public relations than by marketing, which has to focus on relatively short-term results. Though marketing professionals will vigorously contest this proposition, there are convincing reasons why this is true. A corporate-sponsored charity program almost invariably has other dimensions besides selling particular products. The company's image is at issue, not just an ephemeral sales push. Moreover, PR professionals, if they are on the ball, are more adept at self-defense than salespeople. There are risks in strategic philanthropy. The company that makes a serious mistake can look greedy, cruel, and manipulative. Present-day public relations is geared toward getting the most out of such efforts while avoiding pitfalls.

Cause-related marketing should have other payoffs besides marketing—corporate image, internal morale, and community influence.

CALL FOR PHILIP MORRIS

Worthwhile causes and artistic endeavors will, to an increasing extent, attract corporate support because this fits with a good public relations program. That is realistic. It is also not as crass as it might sound at first. By tying in more closely with the corporate world, these nonprofit organizations can have a profound effect on the business realm that they may have feared and shunned.

The Altria Corporation, formerly known as Philip Morris, the multibillion-dollar maker of cigarettes and once a long-time client of mine, has always given lots of money to causes and asked nothing in return. The arts—museums, dance companies, and theater groups—have always been big beneficiaries of Philip Morris.

Paul Goldberger, writing in the *New York Times,* said, "To people in the arts, two of the best words in the English language for more than a generation have been Philip Morris and never mind if the money comes from tobacco."

Symbiotic relationships between causes and companies are here to stay, and will flourish. Companies should approach it in a spirit of enlightened self-interest. Public relations professionals should be sensitive but unapologetic in using associations for promotional purposes.

When the cause is worthy, appropriate, and well chosen, the company—whether it is multinational or a neighborhood business—gets results.

American education is already benefiting—and will benefit more—from cause-related public relations. Corporations have been contributing to education, in various forms, for many years. Sometimes corporations have focused on schools in communities where the company has facilities. In other cases, they have contributed to schools that teach skills the company can use. Still others concentrate on making it possible for the children of employees to get good educations.

On the whole, the growth of cause-related public relations is an excellent development. Such partnerships will be one of the most significant contributions of the 21st-century corporation and small business. And it never would have happened if public relations practitioners hadn't paved the way.

What about the causes themselves? The big ones, like the Red Cross, Salvation Army, Catholic Charities, America's Second Harvest, the Special Olympics, Habitat for Humanity, and Goodwill Industries, are all public relations savvy. There are countless others, however, that lack the PR expertise to guarantee success.

GOODWILL . . . GOOD PR

I learned that Christine Bragale, director of media relations for Goodwill Industries, was going to speak at a *PR News* nonprofit awards breakfast at the National Press Club in Washington near the end of 2005. I was curious. What does a PR practitioner for a charitable organization tell others, particularly when many causes are often under fire for spending too much money on administrative costs. Here's what Bragale, a former Associated Press staffer, said. I offer her thoughts to you because her advice, while addressed to nonprofits, is excellent advice for everyone in PR, whether you work for a big corporation or a small business or small cause, or a local, regional, statewide, or national government.

It is interesting first to note that Goodwill operates differently than many nonprofits. They earn 98 percent of their revenues—with 2 percent coming from financial donations. In 2004, more than 723,000 people benefited from Goodwill's career programs. Every 72 seconds of every business day, Goodwill placed someone into a solid job. Bragale said the following:

> It's a pretty cool statistic, isn't it, but my gut says you did not know it, despite my best efforts. What Goodwill does, what

Habitat for Humanity does, what Special Olympics does should be in the news every day, especially when you consider the collective impact on a community. But doing well doesn't seem newsworthy—reporters want stories that have tension, that involve lies and greed . . . and it's not really what nonprofits are about.

Our role as nonprofit PR practitioners is vital to the long-term viability of our respective organizations.

It is also vital to the long-term viability of everyone reading this book (and those who should be reading this book), no matter where you work.

Bragale said, "Goodwill's founder would think it laughable that the survival of an organization that is 103 years old depends on a handful of PR people. And he would be right."

While working at the AP, Bragale stated the following:

> We were always told that it was better to be second and right, than to be first and wrong.
>
> I think, however, that times have changed at many news outlets. One of my associates has gotten so many corrections in the *New York Times* these last two months that the ombudsman called to ask she call him directly whenever she feels she has a problem with a *Times* reporter. I don't know if ombudsmen make it a habit to reach out to PR people, but I've never heard of this practice before.

Bragale then offered some advice to her colleagues in the nonprofit PR world, advice she could give as a former AP staffer:

> Don't let a journalist get away with being wrong. It's your job to set the record straight—your organization's reputation, maybe even its survival, depends on it. (But do it nicely, I say.)

So what can we do to protect our organization? One word: transparency. If you've made a mistake, admit it. Did a senior official embezzle money? Yes, she did, and as a result we've implemented a whole new set of financial controls. Want to know how much the CEO makes? It's public information, right here on our IRS form 990.

The PR professional has a bird's eye view of the organization, and daily contact with people in all departments at all levels, from the CEO to the case worker to the volunteer to the donor to the program participant. We know how the public perceives us. As communicators, we can and must become a part of the decision-making circle. Assess questionable issues. Question troublesome decisions. Scrutinize business plans and processes. Help steer an organization ethically.

Sometimes my CEO gets mad at me and calls me the voice of doom and gloom. And I just smile and remind him that he pays me to be negative. But I like to think that my questions sometimes cause us to stop and think about the unintended consequences of the decisions we are about to make. And that tough questions help remind us that our purpose here is to help people while at the same time being good stewards of the resources—be they money or clothes—that the public has entrusted to us. That is the key to our integrity and to our survival.

It was refreshing to hear Bragale's comments. It was also refreshing when I learned about a group of students in a public relations class at Oklahoma State University that produced a concert of local bands at the Student Union Theater, November 7, 2005, for the benefit of Hurricane Katrina victims in New Orleans.

Small and big businesses should approach cause-related PR in a spirit of enlightened self-interest. Public relations professionals should be sensitive but unapologetic in using the association for promotional purposes.

17

READ, READ, READ

And Other Ways to Stay Ahead

The title of this chapter is the public relations equivalent to real estate's most important rule—location, location, location. Too many PR practitioners today are too busy in their off-duty hours to read. As a result, they pitch to newspapers and magazines they have never read. PR practitioners should be voraciously inquisitive, eager to learn about everything that is going on, and omnivorous readers.

Today, you don't have to spend more than gas money to get your required fill of information. The local public library carries most publications that are important to PR practitioners. "Gas costs too much," you're saying. Don't worry, there's the Internet. I spend hours each day on the Internet, reading online newspapers or newsletters, or searching for information relating to a client's business

Before the Internet, I was a library buff. I spent many days in the mid-Manhattan branch of the New York Public Library. Currently, I am a few minutes away from an excellent branch of the

Palm Beach County (Florida) library system, and I'm in the periodical section regularly for an hour or two. Most libraries carry all the leading magazines and a large selection of daily newspapers, both local and national. I usually read four to six newspapers every day and skim a couple of dozen magazines each month. Rarely a day goes by when I don't read something of interest to one of the projects I am working on at the time.

Weekly community newspapers also belong on your must-read list. When I published and edited a weekly newspaper in the Hamptons section of New York State, I was amazed by how many people sent in press releases and didn't have a clue what the paper was about.

Today, the Internet never ceases to thrill me and to make life easier for me to keep up to date. I receive daily news digests from a number of newspaper, magazine, and broadcast Web sites. The phenomenal search engine Google sends me daily alerts on as many topics as I choose. My engineer brother is the creator of the Saffir-Simpson Hurricane Scale. *Saffir-Simpson* is on my Google alert list. Wherever and whenever the scale is published, I get an alert from Google with the relevant link (my in-box gets busy during the summer hurricane season).

Some of the items in this book were called to my attention by a Google alert.

In Chapter 15, I write about an interesting new company called Publicity Guaranteed. Here's how I found out about them. On September 26, 2005, the company's parent announced the launch of its new PR business by posting a release on PR Newswire, one of the major press release distribution-to-media companies. Within a couple of hours of its release to media throughout the country, Google sent me an alert and a link where I was able to read the company's complete press release. I then contacted the company for more information.

Take some time each week and browse the Web sites of some of the major newspapers and magazines. Having spent time in the Philippines as a foreign correspondent and, later on, for my work there in PR (see Chapter 20), I was interested in the possible impeachment of the president of the country in 2006. The *New York Times* barely reported on the subject. I got my fill by reading several Manila newspapers' accounts of the events of the day.

Even though the Internet has changed the way public relations is practiced, I urge those seeking to be PR savvy not to give up the printed word. Too many PR people these days have, for the most part, stopped reading printed publications and spend all their time on the Internet. This is wrong, and those who do will pay the price one day. If public relations is important to you, then you must read on and offline.

Here's an unsigned blog I found on a Web site called WXP-news:

> Fifteen years ago, I couldn't have imagined not subscribing to the local newspaper. Waiting for the paper to come each day was an important part of life when I was growing up. Not anymore, I still read the *Dallas Morning News* every day, as I have since childhood, but I don't have to wait for it to be delivered all at once; now the stories are updated as they occur. I don't have to go out in a downpour to get them, and I don't have to deal with throwing away stacks of newsprint every week. I read my news on the Web, and I'm not limited to my local newspaper. I read several major city and specialty dailies, and the only one I have to pay for is the *Wall Street Journal.*

That is exactly what I am afraid of. Do not—repeat—do not stop reading offline! There's no denying that a growing number of people get most of their news from the Internet. Newspaper circulations, indeed, are going down, and they will continue to do so, but they still are an important part of PR. The Internet and printed media should be treated as equals in your reading. Do not take away time from the printed word for the Internet; if you want to rise to the top of the class, you read both. Sometimes there are two sides to a story but only one makes it to the public. And remember, not everything in print is posted on the Internet. You may miss an extremely important piece of information by not reading offline.

INTERNET INACCURACY

When you read information on the Internet, it is critical that you make certain what you're reading is accurate.

The *Tennessean* newspaper ran an Op Ed column in December 2005 about "character assassination." The writer was John Seigenthaler, father of the NBC nightly news anchor. It seems Wikipedia, the popular online free encyclopedia, published "false, malicious" biographical data about the elder Seigenthaler.

Wikipedia reported that Seigenthaler "moved to the Soviet Union in 1971 and returned to the United States in 1984. He started one of the country's largest public relations firms shortly thereafter."

Wikipedia went on to report that he "was thought to have been directly involved in the Kennedy assassinations of both John and his brother Bobby." Seigenthaler said:

At age 78, I thought I was beyond feeling surprise or anger at anything negative anybody said about me. I was wrong. It was infuriating to read that stuff under my name. And it was mind-boggling when my son (the NBC journalist) phoned from New York to say he had discovered the same scurrilous text on two other Web sites, *Reference.com* and *Answers.com.*

They did not know where the information came from except that the writer was a customer of BellSouth Internet.

Seigenthaler could have filed a lawsuit against BellSouth, but federal privacy laws shield the identity of Internet customers. Instead he wrote his Op Ed piece to alert the public, "that Wikepedia is a flawed and irresponsible research tool."

The Seigenthaler biography on Wikipedia has been corrected. Seigenthaler told the *New York Times,* "We live in a universe of new media with phenomenal opportunities for worldwide communications and research, but populated by volunteer vandals with poison-pen intellects."

The lesson here is to be careful when you're reading. If you go public with information found on the Internet, be sure and check it for accuracy. Still, I don't sell Wikipedia short. In the next few years, I believe the company will be a major, credible online source of information, much like encyclopedias when I was growing up.

WHAT YOU SHOULD LOOK FOR

If you're in the bead business, or selling some kind of widgets, it will cost you nothing to ask Google to alert you to (key words) beads or the name of your widget. You may want to Google your competition. It would be very helpful if you get a heads-up on something a competitor is planning ahead of time, and an announcement of this may appear in a newspaper that you do not regularly read.

When you are reading, pay close attention to the various departments of the publications, special sections, and columnists. Look at bylines; most people don't. Learn the deadlines for receiving material.

By keeping up-to-date, you will be better at brainstorming, and you'll be able to react to faster current news events and tie them in with local charities and special events. In 2005, it was a no-brainer for PR-savvy people to tie in with the Hurricanes Katrina, Rita, and Wilma disaster efforts. By reading, you may find a relatively unknown cause that works well with your business, client, or your own nonprofit organization in your area. A human-interest story may give you an idea for a tie-in with your business or cause. A great idea you learn from a San Diego newspaper might work in New England.

During the Tiananmen Square massacre in Beijing, China, I learned from a friend that there were 250 American students at Beijing University. I called my contact at Philip Morris and suggested the corporation charter a plane to pick up the students. Within a half hour, my contact called back and told me the president of the company said, "Do it." In less than an hour, we located a plane big enough to handle the flight. Only delays coming from the bureaucracy in the State Department of our government caused the plan to be aborted.

If you have a client, you should know everything that is going on in the company . . . read all their publications

Trade publications of your client's industry are also extremely important. It's a no-brainer, but you would be surprised how many account executives I came in contact with that didn't read their industry's trade publications.

While reading trade publications, you will find a lot of information about your competitors. Even better, read your competitors' Web sites, check out their press rooms, which are always a great source of information. I find it easier and faster to go to a company's Web site to get a telephone number than going through the telephone-industry information process.

In addition to reading, people working in various places in the organization can be valuable sources. People with resounding titles or big salaries are not always the most valuable sources. Veterans in production, executive assistants, supervisors, clerks in a store, or volunteers to an association can be very helpful. They see the results of management policy in action. And, sometimes, they can warn about things that are about to go wrong. Above all, they are the sources of nitty-gritty detail, which give credibility and texture to stories.

Reading daily will put you ahead of most people in the company who do not read daily, except for, perhaps, the trade publications covering their industry.

If you don't believe me, take it from Harold Burson, the man *PR Week* named "the century's most influential PR figure."

"It's important in this business to relate to people in a way that will cause them to have confidence in you. Part of that is being knowledgeable about a lot of subjects. Do a tremendous amount of reading. Keep up-to-date on business and the news," Burson told the *Bulldog Reporter*.

Burson says he reads three daily newspapers every morning before he gets to the office, and a number of magazines and books each week and month. "There has never been a time in my life when I'm not reading a book," Burson says.

Like Burson, I tell entry-level people to never stop trying to learn.

PR practitioners can find out interesting things from reading and talking to members of the trade press, as well as suppliers and customers. The idea is to keep your eyes and ears open as much as possible, and to always think about the possibilities. That way, when a new development is revealed, public relations can do more than just write a few press releases.

If you're the sole practitioner of your PR firm working out of the guest room in your home, or part of a small PR firm, you should read the public relations trade media. The *Bulldog Reporter* and its sister publications listed in the last chapter of this book, is an excellent source for business- and lifestyle-media pitching tips. They also have a section called "Fast Moves," which reports on staff changes like this:

Associated Press national desk editor Lisa Tolin *(ltolin@ ap.org)* shifts to editor of asap, its forthcoming service for 18- to 34-year-old readers, overseeing business, entertainment, lifestyle and sports coverage.

By reading this item you would not only have learned about the staff change, you would also have learned that the AP has a new special wire for a demographic market that you may be interested in. Incidentally, AP's new service offers articles in print and multimedia formats with audio, video, blogs, and wireless text.

Betty Yarmon's *Party-Line* newsletter is another good source for PR tips. For less than $200 a year, Yarmon sends out more than 1,000 placement tips a year.

Yarmon, a veteran in PR, told me she feels the future of PR has never been brighter:

> There are so many new places for placements: blogs, the Internet, newsletters, etc. Nowadays, it is not the usual newspapers, mags, TV, and radio; sure they are important, but they do not play as important a part; and the new trend is not to just have advertising, but to have it joined by PR placements.

Sharon Dotson of Houston told me she knew nothing about the Internet when she started her PR business, Bayou City Public Relations, in 2001. "By reading some newsletters, I learned a lot," Dotson said. She recommendeds the following newsletters:

- With nearly 25 years in the PR trenches, Bill Stoller's *Free Publicity, the Newsletter for PR Hungry Businesses,* can tell you a lot about how hi-tech changed the face of PR. (See Chapter 9 for more on Stoller.) "He may be teaching the uninitiated about PR, but he also has a lot to teach PR people who believe themselves to be experienced," Dotson said.
- *The Publicity Hound* e-newsletter. "This one is free and it's great. It teaches the new PR on the Internet."

Some PR media have Web sites that are free. You say you can't afford to join the Public Relations Society of America. What you can do, for free, is read the Public Relations Society of America Web site *(www.PRSA.org)*. You may get an idea that will work for you.

Many PR publications offer Webinars to help those who want to help themselves. *PR News,* October 2005, went to cyberspace to tackle the new media beast and educated PR pros on blogs and such. Said one speaker, "Get up on the learning curve. When you live on the edge, sometimes you slip."

In summary, it's essential to know what's going on in your community, region, nationally, and internationally, and in the companies and organizations that may be your client or employer.

O'Dwyers and *PR Week* are other publications where you will find a great deal of useful, current information.

MENTORING

Harold Burson recommends the following:

Find a role model or mentor you can emulate and learn from. Also never stop trying to learn. A lot of entry-level people end up self-training because it's not available from the top—so get into situations that can be learning experiences. For example, volunteer for jobs outside your work responsibility. What you learn will help later.

Equally important is not to be afraid to approach senior-level people. Sure it's a hit or miss—and it takes two to tango. I've picked out people in my career that I thought were bright, and I helped them. But I've also had people come to me saying, "Can I talk to you?" That's the first step.

During my first job while I was still going to college, I worked as a copy boy for the old International News Service. The famed columnist Bob Considine asked me to go across the street to buy him a coffee and doughnut. When I returned he gave me a dollar bill. I told him I was just doing my job and wouldn't take his money. He told me something I've remembered all my life, "Be nice to people on your way up, because they may pass you on your way down."

Here's another quote from Considine that I like:

> Call it vanity, call it arrogant presumption, call it what you wish, but I would grope for the nearest open grave if I had no newspaper to work for, no need to search for and sometimes find the winged word that just fits, no keen wonder over what each unfolding day may bring.

I later worked on assignments with Considine in Dallas and Tokyo. He was my mentor and tears came to my eyes when I attended a memorial service to him in 1975 following his death.

TUNE IN TO THE GRAPEVINE

Without being assigned to the job, a PR practitioner can make points by circulating brief memos commenting on the public relations aspects of recent events in the company or industry. Of course, these comments must have a point and must not be hot air. But when memos are sent out regularly, they can help senior management see that PR functions are more than just wordsmithing. And these memos can help others develop more of a public relations point of view, which can help when decisions are being made and implemented.

One of the benefits of reading is the ability to look ahead. Public relations should be prepared to deal with change. It helps when change does not come as a complete surprise. In a well-run organization where public relations has established the proper weight and status, top management will trust the function enough to share thoughts about long-range plans. In many places, however, top management tries to keep the lid on important plans right up until the last moment. This includes keeping public relations in the dark. That may not be logical and PR professionals may deplore it, but it is the way it goes in the real world. Sometimes in such companies and organizations, new developments are suddenly sprung on public relations, and when the function does not respond instantly with a detailed and effective plan, the critics ask, "What good is public relations anyway?"

Savvy PR professionals should develop sensitive antennae. Tune in to the grapevine. Find out what is happening inside and outside the company. Most times speculation about the future is wrong. But PR practitioners should be aware of the possibilities and spend a few moments thinking about the PR implications. Then, if there is a possibility that a development may be more than idle rumor, public relations should start planning.

18

PR, ADVERTISING, AND JOURNALISM

Synergies and Frictions

The world of public relations is changing, but not necessarily for the good, at least according to one of PR's wise men, Jack O'Dwyer. Since leaving his newspaper job in the 1960s as an advertising/public relations/marketing columnist for the long defunct New York City daily, the *Journal American,* O'Dwyer has been publishing PR-related material. The O'Dwyer Company is in its fourth decade covering, researching, and ranking the PR industry. He has expanded with a monthly magazine, a daily Web site, and directories of PR firms. O'Dwyer's Public Relations News Web site is No. 1 on Google when you search for *original PR reporting.*

O'Dwyer believes that giant advertising agencies are exerting too much influence on public relations companies. In a column he wrote on August 30, 2005, O'Dwyer charged that Omnicom, the parent of PR giants Fleishman-Hillard, Ketchum, Porter Novelli, Broeder, and scores of smaller firms, almost never answers press calls. O'Dwyer wrote:

We think the information-averse policies of Omnicom are damaging to its PR operations, which publicized themselves for decades by pointing to their overall growth rates and leadership in the dozen specialized PR areas such as beauty/fashion, technology, financial, healthcare, food, etc.

Failure to report staff size damages the credibility of the PR firms. Prospective clients want to know the size of the firm they're dealing with.

O'Dwyer believes Omnicom has shifted its annual meeting from New York three years in a row to avoid the press. PR was Omnicom's worst performing sector in the second quarter of 2005, according to O'Dwyer. "Where Omnicom gets these numbers from is a mystery not only to us but security analysts. We don't know how it defines PR. For the fourth straight year, Omnicom has forbidden any of its PR units from releasing fee income or staff totals."

When I worked for the Richard Weiner agency before it was sold to Omnicom and became Porter Novelli, we were thrilled to release our figures because we were growing significantly every year. Omnicom's growth rate appears to come heavily through acquisitions, says O'Dwyer.

It is inevitable that people in the client organization will persistently act as if public relations is identical to advertising. These people will insist that releases and articles be written as if they were ad copy. They will expect that public relations be tested by the same tests applied to advertising.

Public relations can work closely with advertising, supplement it, augment it, and even replace it in certain cases. But public relations is not advertising. For example, let's look at the concept of testing. Advertisements carry repeat messages in select media and useful yardsticks have been developed to test the impact and retention of these ads. Public relations must be held up against different yardsticks.

Clients should remember that public relations has power because it is *not* paid for, at least not like advertising is paid for. Material that appears in news columns has more credibility than ads.

It's a no-brainer as to which is better: a PR-driven news story in the Sunday edition of the local newspaper or an advertisement that is buried in the peek-a-boo-I-see-you confusion that marks most Sunday newspapers.

Public relations cannot be judged by the size of the story or the number of minutes of broadcast time. Clients and small-business owners should understand the principles of public relations, at least to the extent of avoiding confusion with advertising. Clients should hold public relations accountable—but accountable to realistic standards.

Public relations professionals set themselves up as targets for this falsely premised assessment when they do not make sure that all relevant parties understand that public relations is different from advertising. Sure, in a broad sense, public relations and advertising aim at the same objectives—as do manufacturing, research, finance, and every other department. But the subgoals of public relations are different, and so are the means public relations uses.

Public relations, sometimes, can replace advertising, but advertising can never replace public relations. Advertising, we know, is paid for by the company, association, business, or individual. The ad is the partial message of the advertiser. In PR, what is read or heard in the media is from a third party.

PR/ADVERTISING RIVALRY

For a small business or nonprofit organization short of money, public relations is the only way to go. Publicity generates a lot of credibility and can always be produced at a lower cost.

There will always be a rivalry between advertising and PR. That is healthy—as long as it stops short of paranoia.

Melding advertising and public relations is often a painful process, punctuated with shrieks of anguish and growls of unfriendliness. The biggest problems involve people and money.

Public relations and advertising forces should work closely together. This cooperation can and should be expedited by structural arrangements. When it is necessary, the two disciplines should be given the same information, brought in on projects at the same time, and invited to the same meetings.

However, just getting public relations and advertising people to sit down with each other does not bring about fruitful interaction. The road to cooperation is often blocked by misunderstanding, mistrust, and rivalry.

Peter Wengryn, president and CEO of VMS, explains this very clearly:

> One of the biggest challenges to integrating marketing communications is corporate structure. Public relations, marketing, and advertising groups frequently live in different departments. Companies often have public relations and advertising from different companies. Efforts to track and demonstrate results are made in isolation. Aligning the advertising, marketing, and public relations functions is necessary to ensure a clear and consistent message is being delivered to chosen publics.

Wengryn told me that the Whirlpool Company is a good example of integrated marketing. The Whirlpool-brand marketing team includes public relations, advertising, new business development, and marketing. "Any suggestion from one discipline has to be extended to the others for consideration," Wengryn said.

PR IGNORANCE

Everyone knows, more or less, what advertising is, but there is ignorance and confusion about public relations, even among people who should be better informed. It is, unfortunately, not uncommon for an advertising-agency account supervisor, meeting with the client and the PR agency, to demand that the PR agency place publicity in precise coordination with the ad campaign launch, and to expect that the PR material will parrot the key selling lines of the advertising. And worse, the client is not up to speed on public relations either, so PR practitioners have a problem with the client and the advertising agency.

When this happens, the public relations team is forced into a defensive posture. First, the team ends up conducting an instant adult-education course on public relations; second, the team has to explain why they cannot do what others expect them to do. This is not a comfortable position. It leaves PR practitioners open to suspicion that they are making excuses in advance for lack of performance.

Advertising should have called in public relations to sit at the same table from the early brainstorming stage through the campaign launch. And public relations literacy should be a job requirement for corporate executives and advertising professionals.

CODEPENDENT RIVALS

Not only do PR people have to put up with advertising, they have to coexist with the world of journalism.

The two fields have existed as codependent rivals since the advent of modern PR in the 1920s, explains Edward Wasserman, a professor of journalism ethics at Washington & Lee University:

The relationship has since softened into a grudging mutual reliance. PR people have the information, journalists have the outlets; communications requires both. Journalists view PR people the way spouses see their in-laws: grateful for the gift, wary of the givers. To the PR side, the journalist is the son-in-law, both undeserving and indispensable.

Wasserman, in a column he wrote for the *Miami Herald* and *Palm Beach Post,* September 6, 2005, which also ran on the Knight-Tribune wire service, said he thought more people are going into public relations than journalism:

> Why PR appeals now to young potential reporters no doubt has to do with the heavy cloud of economic gloom hovering over the news business. It also reflects a wish, as a Palestinian journalism student who was going into PR told me his aim was to do something "active"—to make things happen instead of reacting to events. Students come back from summer PR internships with exciting tales of scanning the next day's papers for stories they helped bring about.

Wasserman believes PR is promising something else to the young and impressionable: a role in contemporary affairs that's way beyond message creation, brand maintenance, or advocacy. The PR professional is proposed as a senior counselor not just on what is persuasive and effective, but on what is right—as chief integrity officer.

"PR appeals powerfully to the longing of the young not for a job but for a mission. Once, that's what journalism promised, and should promise again," believes Wasserman.

As James Lukaszewski, a PR practitioner who consults on such matters, was quoted in Knight-Ridder newspaper, September 12, 2005, "The primary goal of public relations will be to create an environment of integrity within organizations."

Okay, you're fresh out of college and you think you know everything there is to know about journalism and public relations, but you are undecided where you should begin. You would like to be another Woodward or Bernstein and emulate their reportorial successes in the Watergate era, but you're concerned about the growing public mistrust of the media. PR sounds appealing but you don't like the label *flack,* which is sometimes used to describe a practitioner of public relations. Let's take a look at how I got into the PR business.

I studied journalism and public relations in college and worked as a copy boy for a now defunct wire service. The copy boy experience served me well when I entered the Marine Corps. I was given a specialty classification of combat correspondent, which got me assigned to the Parris Island weekly newspaper for one year and public information (PR) in my second year. Because of my service-related newspaper experience, after my discharge I was quickly able to land a reporter's job that took me to Dallas and Tokyo for a combined total of six years. With that experience, I was ready for public relations. Having worked in the media, I knew the media and that, in my judgment, is the best experience for someone going into PR.

In a small agency, you learn faster because most of the time you're involved in everything from brainstorming to media relations to stuffing envelopes. In a larger agency, an account executive's workload is limited to certain areas, as discussed in Chapter 3.

Howard Rubenstein advises today's up-and-comers to not fall in love with money:

> Fall in love with what you do to earn money. Be honorable and you will earn a great living. For example, don't let a client blind you with gold dust and ask you to do improper things. Too often—and it doesn't matter if you're new in the business or not—a client will say, "We want to cover this up. Why don't you say and do this for us?" My advice is don't do it. Explain

that it will hurt the client if you issue a false statement or spin out of control. Also, the media will be skeptical about even the good things you do. Over the years, I have advised clients not to take that path. I advise all PR people not to succumb to the temptation of a big client trying to force you to do something.

Rubenstein also advises not to face down the client directly:

> Use your PR skills and talk them out of it. I talked some of my biggest clients out of things, and it has worked because I was never hired to be a yes man. I'd sooner drop a client than do something that will stick with me afterwards. Remember the way you practice business stays with you longer than the clients you practice it with.

Rubenstein, in his 70s, puts in 60 to 70 hours each week.

I predict that the similarities between public relations and advertising will become more important than the differences, and the result will be a gradual blending of the specialties.

Right now, in most cases, the two do not mix. An advertising agency and a public relations function may work under the same roof and under the same company name, and serve the same clients, but they have their separate organizations.

19

EVALUATING THE
PR PROGRAM

The Nuts and Bolts of Measurement

Once you've developed a PR program, the next step is to ask, "How am I doing?" It's not an easy question to answer.

It's easy to evaluate advertising or direct mail programs; you can compare them to previous programs. Also, sophisticated methods have been developed to test the impact and retention of advertising messages. A very successful fundraising letter for a political candidate may result in a 2 or 3 percent response with checks. If your President's Day sale advertising brought customers into your store—more than you had the previous year—the advertising worked.

Public relations does its job differently than advertising and must be measured differently.

In PR, one asks, "Compared to what?" This is the key question in evaluating a PR program. Public relations does not fit into a convenient slot. It contributes to sales (or at least it should), but it does not generate the concrete numbers that can be used to assess sales performance, hand out bonuses, and set quotas.

Currently, we have useful research resources to help us shape and direct public relations programs, yet we have been unable to develop reliable and universally accepted means of measuring what public relations does.

When PR professionals raise this argument about the difficulties in evaluation, it is sometimes derided as a cop-out. Mean-spirited people make snide comments like, "The flacks resist testing because they are selling blue sky." In the face of this, PR professionals must be able to do more than simply fend off unwelcome evaluation measures. The best approach is to build commonsense, evaluative criteria into the program.

These criteria will vary from company to company, nonprofit to nonprofit, and program to program. Here are some issues to consider when crafting an evaluation procedure that works.

SET GOALS

What is the program supposed to accomplish? This, of course, is a fundamental question, not only for evaluation, but for planning and implementation of a program. It goes to the very heart of the public relations effort, so it might be reasonable to think that the goals, long and short term, are spelled out before the program starts. In a surprising number of cases, public relations lacks clear objectives. It becomes a process that seems to be carried on for its own sake. Vagueness makes it easier to get away with lackluster work.

A lack of clear goals is a malady besetting other corporate disciplines. Customer service is an example. In 2005, I spent countless days, weeks, and months talking to customer service and technical representatives from call centers in India about problems with my new Dell computer. It became a nightmare. The company finally replaced my lemon.

Training is another example. Training can last for years and cost a lot in time and effort, but not much is accomplished because nobody knows the goals of the training. Everybody knows, however, that training is something you have to do.

When setting up a PR program, as well as a customer service and training program, it is important to ask, "When this program ends, how will things be different from the way they were when the program started?" The search for answers to this question can be a forging of useful goals. The goals can usually not be quantified precisely. But in the case of public relations, it should be possible to make statements like these:

- People who are important to us will know our name and what we do.
- Our new products and services will be familiar to more prospects.
- The positions of our company, nonprofit, retail business, or branch of government—local, regional, or national—will be understood and respected, even if the positions do not receive universal acceptance.

DON'T COUNT PRESS RELEASES

The number of press releases sent out is not a useful criterion of effectiveness. Sending out 964 releases all around the country by itself will not make it. The number of messages delivered has some value as a yardstick—but with qualifications. Sometimes, a PR department or agency can mount an intriguing presentation featuring the number of impressions registered on various populations or markets. "Two hundred thousand people read our story in the *Dallas Morning News*." This is a legitimate means of measurement. However, it may not give the evaluators much feel for the depth of the impressions made. There should be an agreement on the media that are most desirable. Impressions can be weighed with regard to the authority and aura of the median.

Here are some questions to ask that will help evaluate the effectiveness of press releases and other tactics:

- Is the quality and nature of the publication or media outlet on target?
- Do the headlines, subheadlines, captions, photos, or anything special other than copy gain attention? For broadcast or video placements, how are they introduced?
- Does the story contain the key copy points from the campaign strategy?
- Are the key copy points in a good location in the placement?
- Is the length long enough to communicate the message?
- How timely is the placement in relation to the campaign schedule? Great placement, but the sale was yesterday.
- Is the placement/video useful for merchandising purposes such as direct mailings, management presentations, or publishing on a Web site?

These questions offer a sensible combination of scientific measurement and common sense, and they serve as a framework for the PR evaluation process.

WORK WITH OTHERS AND TAKE RISKS

All the impressions in the world will not help if the PR program is not working in harmony with the other relevant departments, notably advertising, marketing, and legal. Of course, if PR stood alone, measurement would be easier.

A PR program's activities and accomplishments cannot be weighed in a vacuum. They must be evaluated as to how they fit in with the initial objectives and the agreed-on process.

A play-it-safe PR program never makes any mistakes—except the biggest mistake of all: futility. If assessment focuses too much on things that can go wrong, it will stultify creativity. Things can go wrong in any area of the business. Risk is everywhere.

Public relations practitioners should take appropriate risks and be prepared to defend these risks. PR practitioners should ensure that risks and mistakes are evaluated in the context of what was intended and what is being accomplished overall. Here is an analogy. A company spends years investing a significant amount of money developing a new product. The product goes on the market. There are some problems and failures. The company recalls some products and fulfills some guarantees. But the company does not junk the new product program because of these bugs. The more ambitious and innovative the program, the greater likelihood of problems, especially right after the program kicks off. Evaluation of the PR program should assume that there will be problems, and the evaluation should judge how well these problems are handled.

COUNT CLIPS THE RIGHT WAY

The most basic—and probably the most antiquated—evaluation of a PR program is counting newspaper clippings, or clips, as they are often called. After a campaign, all the clips are assorted by date, listing publication names, circulations, and dates of publications. Using circulation numbers, the PR person adds the average number of readers and comes up with a final total of what is called *impressions,* as if everyone reading the newspaper read the placement. The same can be done with broadcast media using data of a show's viewing or listening audience.

David Michaelson and Toni Griffin, in a paper called "A New Model for Media Content Analysis" written for the Institute for Public Relations, calls clip counting the thud factor, or the volume of noise generated when the book of bound clips hits a table.

The results of counting clippings contains no insights and no references as to whether the PR strategy was implemented, and leaves it to the reader to draw judgments.

Here is what should be added to make the analysis more meaningful:

- *Publication or media outlet.* The quality and nature of the publication or media outlet, with respect to the target audience
- *Information highlights.* The headline, subhead lines, captions, pictures, or anything special, other than copy, that would gain attention or communicate
- *Placement copy points.* The extent to which a placement contains key copy points within the placement
- *Information location.* The communications influence of the location of key copy points within the placement
- *Placement length.* The influence of placement length in communicating the message to the target audience
- *Placement timing.* How timely the placement is, relative to the campaign schedule
- *Merchandisability.* Those qualities that make a placement useful for other purposes, such as direct mailings, management presentations, a spot on a Web site, and lobbying

The assessment process above uses four measurements: volume, gross impressions, conformity with strategy, and quality of placements. These are reasonable criteria. However, they are not the be-all and end-all of evaluating the total contribution of a good PR campaign. When properly used, public relations makes a substantial contribution to strategic thinking and planning, and this cannot be measured by volume. Good public relations makes everybody in the organization better at saying and doing things in a way that enhances the public image of the organization. An effective PR operation can make the difference between survival and debacle when misfortune strikes.

Nevertheless, within limits, these yardsticks are helpful in providing an idea of what the function is doing and how well it is doing it. Public relations practitioners make a mistake when they scorn such measuring devices because they are not accurate. No measuring device is perfectly accurate. Besides, the PR industry—by its recent emphasis on the scientific method—has invited this type of scrutiny.

GET INVOLVED

Public relations practitioners should agree to cooperate with the evaluation process. The important thing is for PR practitioners to be involved with the process from the beginning, rather than resisting it. When the PR function is involved in setting up the assessment machinery, that machinery will work more fairly and practically.

When building and running an evaluation program, it is important to have everybody understand how much of the program is objective measurement and how much is subjective measurement. Volume is quantifiable; gross impressions are softer measurements, but they are accepted as long as they do not stand alone.

When we move on to other methods, we move further away from precision. *On strategy* is a judgment call in many cases. A blatant departure from strategy is not debatable, but most cases of possible divergence from strategy are more subtle.

There is even more subjectivity when judging the quality of a placement. In general, certain shows and publications are considered the crème de la crème of the business. But to reach a certain audience with a certain message, a story in *Wired* may be better than a story in the *Washington Post*.

Subjective measurements are likely to be more important than the most quantitative ones. Quality of placement—most people would agree—is more important than simple volume.

So who makes the judgment calls? Line management is apt to insist that it should be the ultimate judge. After all, line management has the responsibility of running the business or organization. Public relations professionals retort that others do not understand the subtleties of the profession, so they are the only ones capable of realistic assessment. Line managers retort that this would be like putting the fox in charge of the hen coop.

Neither side should win this argument. The evaluation of a public relations program should not be altogether in the hands of nonprofessionals. The craft may not be as complicated as nuclear physics, but it requires understanding and insight. Nor should PR practitioners be given unchecked freedom to assess themselves. Even with the best will in the world, those within the craft will be tempted to slant the results.

COMPARE COSTS

Another legitimate yardstick for measuring the results of a public relations program is to compare the benefits of spending on the PR program with alternative uses. The evaluation asks, "What else could we do with the resources?" Public relations practitioners should welcome this measurement—if the question is applied fairly. Unfairness comes in when the evaluators digress into talking about how other objectives could be accomplished.

The typical alternative to public relations is advertising, of course. "For what we spend on public relations we could buy an ad." That statement may be accurate—but the argument is based on the premise that advertising and public relations achieve the same objectives. Public relations professionals set themselves up as targets for this falsely premised assessment when they do not make sure that all relevant parties understand that public relations is different from advertising, and important in its own right.

Sure, in a broad sense, public relations and advertising aim at the same objectives. But the subgoals of public relations are different, and so are the means public relations uses. The evaluation should never be based on the notion that something else could have been done with the money. There has to be a clear understanding of what public relations does, along with an agreement that it is worth doing. When that understanding exists, it is legitimate and useful to judge the program through informed speculation about alternative uses of resources. One prevailing error in evaluation—in public relations as well as advertising—is to judge by the artistic criteria of insiders, rather than by results. Advertising people often toast each other, and confer awards on each other, for advertising that they like but that does not sell the product. Often they like it because it is different, or daring, or titillating. They are bored with advertising, so they go wild over stuff that seems to flout the rules, even if the ad does not do what it is supposed to do. Nearly every day I see a television commercial and ask, "What was that all about? What are they selling?" Many advertising agency art directors put more emphasis on winning awards for out-of-this-world creativity than servicing their clients.

The same thing happens among PR insiders. When a PR practitioner scores a clever coup by getting a story on network news, other PR professionals applaud the PR practitioner as a genius because they know how tough it was to get the story on. However, the actual story may not do much good. Perhaps it would have been far more cost effective to get a number of stories in other more conventional media. But this does not thrill the insiders.

THE IDEAL WAY TO EVALUATE PR

In the final analysis, the best evaluation of the public relations function should be done by a task force comprised of PR professionals, people who work closely with PR (e.g., marketers), and senior managers who have no particular experience with public relations but who have sound judgment and common sense.

The most important consideration in deciding who does the judging is attitude. Individuals who resent or oppose the whole idea of public relations should not be assessing its effectiveness. The judgment that public relations is a useful function should be made at the time it is adopted. Once that battle has been won, the fight should not be carried on in guerilla skirmishes. This ruins the evaluation process and diverts energies that could be used better elsewhere.

If you are a do-it-yourselfer, ask people around you such as customers, suppliers, relatives, and friends to help you evaluate results.

In 2005, one of the worst PR ideas was letting Donald Trump on stage at the Emmys in a pair of overalls to sing the theme song to *Green Acres.* I can't believe that was on strategy. Sure, a lot of people saw him. But did it do any good?

Or how about the fictional practitioner we mentioned earlier who scored a clever coup in getting a story on network television. What good did it do? If the segment had nothing to do with the client's goals and was not on strategy, it would have been far more cost effective to get stories in the local community weekly newspaper that most people read cover to cover. But this does not thrill the insiders.

The evaluation process should be carried forward with the understanding that public relations is an integral part of telling a story. The purpose of an assessment, then, is not to give a thumbs-up or thumbs-down to an activity, but rather to make it more effective, more coherent, and more cost effective. When evaluation is rigorous but fair and soundly based, public relations has nothing to fear. The process is a healthy one.

20

LEARN FROM EXPERIENCE
Mistakes You Shouldn't Make

Like most people, I've probably made every mistake along the way that one could make. Here are two public relations success stories that didn't have happy endings. There's a lot that can be learned from them.

THE MAKING OF A PRESIDENT

I once developed and implemented a public relations program for a foreign politician that cost very little money and resulted in great success. It also paved the way for my client to become arguably the richest man on the planet while I lost money for my work.

Far-fetched? Off-the-wall? Truth, we all know, is sometimes stranger than fiction. I tell this story not to pat myself on the back, but to point out all the things I learned from this nightmarish episode in my life. While I succeeded in my mission beyond all imaginings, I'm not happy with the ending, but I am smarter for it all. Let me explain.

In the early 1960s, I was retained by a young Filipino senator named Ferdinand Marcos and his attractive wife Imelda (yes, the infamous shoe lady). I was even younger than my client. Marcos was very clear about the assignment he gave me: Make him president of the Philippines, and make his wife the first lady.

I had just started my own public relations firm in New York. Having no clients and only a couple of years experience, I was thrilled with the call I got from a Filipino friend in Manila who said he had a client for me.

Two years earlier, I had returned from the Far East where I worked as a foreign correspondent for International News Service, an American news agency owned by the Hearst organization. I knew the Philippines, having covered a number of stories there.

I sat with the Marcoses for days in their modest home in a walled residential area of Manila and listened to fascinating tales of his heroism in World War ll as well as a long list of other accomplishments. I didn't know at the time, but most of the stories were lies. (Do due diligence at the outset and question your client.)

For seven days, I was taken in by the charming, ambitious couple. Imelda, a former beauty queen who claimed to have sung for General Douglas MacArthur during the war, was a gracious hostess. I bounced Ferdinand Junior, "Bong Bong," and daughter Imee on my knee, dined on roast pig, and drank wine. Today, Bong Bong is a member of the Philippine Congress.

I listened in awe to Marcos's tales of his wartime valor as a guerilla officer alongside American soldiers; his capture and torture by the Japanese; and his commendations from General MacArthur who, Marcos noted proudly, once said that Bataan would have fallen much sooner had it not have been for Marcos's courage.

I heard the saga of how he was convicted of murder while a student, refused a pardon, scored top grade in his bar examination while out on bail, and then was acquitted by the supreme court in the Philippines, which at that time was an American court, after arguing his own appeal before the bench.

Above all, I heard about his political ambitions.

The Marcoses became comfortable with me and soon were convinced of my skills in public relations and my contacts with the media. Whatever little money they said they had, it would be used for the campaign. I would be compensated with at least two big public relations accounts he would get for my fledgling PR business. (Don't work for promises only; put the terms and conditions of your work in writing and get it signed by your client.)

How refreshing it was for me to hear Marcos talk about democracy in Asia and to listen to his pledge to clean up the graft and corruption that had existed in his country ever since it won its independence. I was convinced he would go down in history as a great president.

It would not be an easy job. Ferdinand Marcos was not exactly a household name outside of his home in a northern province. The media had never thought of him as a potential presidential candidate. The president at the time, Diosdado Macapagal, hoped to run again and was not in any serious trouble.

I knew the overall goals. I outlined my public relations objectives and strategy, and the tactics to accomplish it.

My strategy—I called it the Good Housekeeping Seal campaign—was to establish the Marcos image in the Philippines by executing most of the tactics in the United States. In those days, no country and no people loved America and everything about America the way the Filipinos did. If you made it in America, you could make it anywhere, certainly in the Philippines.

Marcos in New York

It seems like only yesterday when I paraded Imelda and Ferdinand around New York City, visiting major newspaper and magazine editorial boards along the way. Both gave interviews to every journalist I was able to come up with who had an interest in the Philippines.

At speeches I arranged, at colleges and the Overseas Press Club of America, he moved audiences to the edge of their seats with his stirring remarks.

It all worked. The trips to the United States were a great success. Daily front page articles, many with banner headlines, ran in newspapers throughout the Philippines for weeks, covering the couple's every personal appearance.

Back home, the relatively obscure senator was treated like a chief of state traveling abroad.

Having heard Marcos's incredible—though, unknown to me, untrue—life story, I felt a biography was a must. Marcos was ahead of me, or at least he thought so. He had a Filipino writer and a publishing house ready to publish his biography. Bad idea, I told him. It didn't meet my Good Housekeeping Seal standards. A Filipino writing about another Filipino would not be treated as big news. I wanted a top American author and I wanted the book published in the United States by an important publishing house. After a lengthy search, I found the writer I wanted: Hartzell Spence, a best-selling and highly respected author, and long-time editor of the armed forces newspaper *Stars & Stripes*. Next, I needed a prestigious publishing company. I choose McGraw-Hill.

Marcos hired Spence for $15,000 and made a commitment to purchase 10,000 books at $2 a book from McGraw-Hill, equaling $35,000 in total expenses.

It was Spence's book *For Every Tear a Victory* that gave Marcos a ring of validity and authenticity. Never in world history has a political campaign been conducted on one issue—a book—as it was in Marcos's case in 1965. Most everyone in the Philippines read it. There were editions covering every language. And for those who couldn't read, but could still vote, there was the movie made from the book. The White House, our CIA, the State Department, and influential members of Congress (and me) bought everything in the book hook, line, and sinker. After all, Spence was a respected journalist.

Most of the U.S. major newspapers accepted the book as gospel. The campaign became a one-issue campaign.

President Macapagal, who had originally learned about me from my friend who had introduced me to Marcos, charged that Marcos paid huge sums of money to Spence to write the book in a scheme organized by an American public relations agent. Marcos, however, maintained steadfastly that he had nothing to do with the book. The book became the number one issue of the campaign.

Marcos threatened to have me killed if I revealed any of the details of my work for him.

I kept Marcos's secret because I believed in him. And I kept the secret after two agents of President Macapagal flew to New York and offered to buy my story and letters I had from Marcos for $50,000. At the time, I was unhappy with Marcos because I had yet to earn any money from him; but I still believed that he could be a great leader, a supporter of democracy in Asia, and friend of the United States. I would do nothing to hurt that in exchange for the money offered to me.

Marcos defeated the incumbent president in the 1965 campaign by 670,000 votes. He was born, of course, in the Philippines but was definitely made in the U.S.A. Marcos was reelected once and served for 8 years legally and then tore up the constitution and stayed in power as a dictator for another 12 years.

Four years after he was elected, Marcos took over the Spence book from McGraw-Hill and, through the World Publishing Company of New York and Cleveland, printed an updated edition of the book with the title changed to *Marcos of the Philippines,* still authored by Spence.

A former Filipino senator who became a foreign minister in a subsequent administration called *For Every Tear a Victory* "the infamous book written in an attempt to disguise with false hyperbole the fake character of Marcos's political career."

Author Sterling Seagrove, in his book *The Marcos Dynasty,* wrote the Marcos book had a powerful impact:

> It was Spence more than anyone else who gave the heroic Marcos legend a ring of validity, when his biography, *For Every Tear a Victory,* was published . . . Soon the most respected journals in America were repeating the gospel according to Spence, quoting long passages or summarizing his assertions as if they were palpable facts. After that, who was to challenge the authenticity of the Marcos legend?

During that time, the Marcoses reportedly became multibillionaires. I never got a PR account for my business and I wasn't reimbursed for all my expenses. (Invoice clients monthly for all out-of-pocket expenses.) Marcos, meanwhile, decided it was best not to communicate with me anymore.

Today, Ferdinand Marcos is dead. Imelda returned to the Philippines from exile and lives extravagantly in Manila.

And I have a souvenir of the whole affair: a copy of *For Every Tear a Victory.* It is signed by Hartzell Spence with the notation, "To Lenny, who also suffered."

Going on eBay

In the summer of 2005, I had an idea to finally make some money from my Marcos experience. I put together a package of seven letters and a cablegram sent to me by Marcos showing how he rose to power. I posted them on the Internet-auction site eBay.

I e-mailed the Philippine media. *The Philippine Daily Enquirer* ran a story but the article listed the documents as "alleged" and "purporting to be," which I believe hurt their salability, though I got well over 1,000 hits on the Internet.

The letters did not sell. (Don't believe the old saying, "I don't care what you write about me as long as you get the name right.")

One other thing hurt the package's salability. The country was immersed in impeachment talk and calls for resignation of the current president, Gloria Macapagal-Arroyo, the daughter of the man whom Marcos defeated for the presidency. (Always check the calendar in advance of planning an event.)

I tried again unsuccessfully in the spring of 2006 to sell the letters on eBay. Page Six, the people section in the *New York Post,* ran something about the listing but nothing in the Philippines. Remembrances of a dictator don't sell.

DON'T GET MAD AT THE MEDIA

From my experience, one of the best tips I can give public relations practitioners, do-it-yourselfers, business owners, politicians, and everyone else, is don't pick a fight with the media.

In 1978, I started a daily newspaper in New York City to compete against the *New York Times, New York Post,* and *Daily News.* I called it the *Trib.* I was its editor-in-chief and publisher; my editor was a former editor of *Newsweek* magazine and numerous big-city newspapers. Our board of directors had some big guns. Its members, at one time or another, included a former U.S. senator (Jim Buckley), a former secretary of the treasury (William Simon), a well-known attorney who would become the head of the SEC and CIA (Bill Casey), and the head of a giant New Jersey construction company who would become secretary of labor (Ray Donovan). The stockholders weren't shabby either, for example, Joe Coors, the beer baron, an oil-man friend of the Bushes, and some Wall Street types, as well as Donovan and Simon. The man who would become president of the United States—George Bush the elder—

helped me raise money. More than 140 editorial and businesspeople, including three Pulitzer Prize winners, joined our staff.

There was no World Wide Web available to get the word out. It's hard to think today how we were able to manage years ago or how we would have fared if the Internet had existed along with today's 24-hour news cycle. Because we had a limited advertising budget, most of the *Trib*'s resources went into public relations. I retained two PR agencies for the work. And I worked with them very closely. Our few advertising dollars went to limited television, bus advertising, and billboards. We practiced all the PR principles in this book to alert the public to the first new newspaper in New York in decades.

A month or so before our first issue, I held an open-house reception (for PR purposes, of course) to show off our new offices, our new computer system, and our newly furnished newsroom. We were the first New York newspaper with computers. Remember, this was 1978.

One of the attendees was Arthur Ochs (Punch) Sulzberger, the publisher of the *New York Times* from 1963 to 1992. I took Sulzberger on a tour around our one-acre-sized office. He was astonished with our workplace, which was more modern than his. You can bet it was a thrill for me when, after viewing computer monitors on everyone's desk, Sulzberger told me, "We're going to be computerized later this year . . . and renovate our newsroom." Earlier, Rupert Murdoch had praised me and the *Trib*'s concept in a major speech he delivered at the Overseas Press Club of America in New York.

During a speech I made at the same club, a few months before our first issue, I was highly critical of my three competitors, particularly the *Times*. (My first mistake.) I had to, I thought. Why else was I starting a newspaper? Virtually every major newspaper in the country ran lengthy articles about the *Trib*, before and after our first issue. The *Washington Post* and *Wall Street Journal* ran so many stories—some a page and a page-and-a-half in length—one would have thought they owned a piece of the *Trib*. All the national magazines wrote about us. Television also gave us substantial coverage.

Prior to our first issue, the *Times* did not write one line about the first new newspaper in New York City for many decades. Not even a line in its advertising column. On January 9, we printed and sold out 260,000 newspapers by 9 AM. Once more, we received widespread national media coverage. But no *New York Times*, even though the *Times*, the so-called newspaper of record, has published a box on its front page for years with the line, "All the News That's Fit to Print." Starting a new newspaper, with hundreds of people involved, including high-profile newsmaker board members and stockholders, all operating from a skyscraper building in midtown Manhattan called the *Trib*, was apparently not news that was "fit to print."

We ceased publishing in early April (that's a story for another book). I gathered our 100-plus staff together and told them the news. The next day the *Times* finally acknowledged our existence. They ran their first story about the *Trib*—a story about our demise and a photograph of me telling the staff it was all over. The other newspapers did likewise. All three newspapers wrote condolences to us on their editorial pages.

Years later, someone else started a newspaper in New York, without the heavyweights we had involved in the *Trib*. The *Times*, with a new executive editor, published lengthy articles about the new paper before its first issue, the day after its first issue, and periodic update articles in the weeks and months that followed.

Al Neuharth, the key architect of turning the Gannett newspaper chain into a billion-dollar media conglomerate, was interested in what we did. In fact, he told me years later that he got the inspiration for starting *USA Today* from the *Trib*.

My message here is to be careful when starting fights with the media. Patrick Parrish, a journalism and public relations veteran who was once my editor, puts it nicely: "Don't fight with anyone who buys newsprint by the truck load and ink by the drum."

Here I go again. I'm not following my own advice by telling this story.

You can e-mail me at *Lenpr@bellsouth.net* to see if the *Times* writes anything about this book. Punch Sulzberger, who wished me well in my offices, has been replaced as publisher by his son, Arthur Jr., and there's a new executive editor.

21

THE FUTURE OF PUBLIC RELATIONS

What Now?

We're still in the infancy of the new millennium. So what role will public relations play as the 21st century progresses?

PR will be bigger than it has ever been. More and more people will become PR literate. Public relations will play a big role in our lives and we will be better off for it.

Twenty years ago, there were no such things as do-it-yourself public relations, guaranteed placements, blogging, and the like. In fact, most people didn't even know what public relations was. In my last book on PR, I dedicated the book to my children by writing, "Now, finally you can answer your friends' question, 'What does your father do?'" Today, they not only know what public relations is, they're practicing it—quite well, thank you—in their own careers. I have already told you about my daughter Michelle. My son Andrew, the founder of the Cinema Society, which is the host of V.I.P. attendee-only movies before their general release, was featured prominently, with photo, in a *New York Times* article on April 23, 2006, and, oftentimes, in numerous publications around the country.

As the Internet grows, and as more and more small business people and advocates of a wide range of causes become PR literate, more and more people are going to follow their dreams. Public relations, now truly coming of age, will drive everyone's dreams in the future.

Even though technology and the Internet are making the future of public relations look brighter than at any time in history, they haven't changed the fundamentals.

I wrote an Op Ed piece for the *Bulldog Reporter's Daily 'Dog* that spotlighted the importance of returning to relationship building. It ran on the Internet on January 18, 2006.

For this book, as you have already noted, I asked some of the leaders in PR—those on the firing lines today, those I have great respect for—for their views.

Here are some more—the thoughts Howard Rubenstein passed on to me. I respect him. I agree with him. His firm, Rubenstein Associates, has hundreds of clients served by a staff of close to 200 from offices in New York. Donald Trump is a former client. By the way, he lost Trump as a client to Rubenstein Public Relations, a firm that is run by his son Richard.

Clearly, the Internet is the single biggest technological development to affect the public relations industry during the past 50 years. It has changed the speed with which stories travel around the world, compressing the news cycle in ways that were unimaginable only a few short years ago. The flow of information and reactions to it are today virtually instantaneous, putting tremendous pressure on PR professionals to make every communications opportunity count, according to Rubenstein.

Rubenstein is smart enough to know that technology hasn't changed the fundamentals that have been in place for decades. The techniques and strategies that practitioners should use to frame a story, the honest and ethical advice and counsel they should offer clients, and the expertise and knowledge they need for success, as outlined in previous chapters, remain the same. If anything, these qualities and skills are more important now than ever and will be so in the years ahead. In sum, technology has changed how PR is practiced but hasn't affected what PR does or why it is important, and that is essential in the future.

"In an information age that is supported and fueled by technological advances, it is only natural that public relations will continue to grow in importance and influence," Rubenstein told me.

After hearing from Rubenstein, I started thinking about my start in public relations.

When I first started in PR, I had a journalism background and, as a result, a leg up on my contemporaries. The main thing was I knew how to write and how to work with the media, which are two important essentials one needs for PR success.

On my return from foreign news reporting, I joined a small PR agency in New York. One of my first jobs was to promote McDonald's Hamburger University, an assignment given to us by the Chicago-based PR firm, Golin Harris, which celebrated its 50th anniversary in 2005.

I look to see the Rubenstein and Golin Harris firms around for a long time.

READING THE PUBLIC MIND

I asked agency founder Al Golin, one of the few practitioners to win a Gold Anvil award from the Public Relations Society of America, his thoughts for the future, and for advice to those in or going into public relations. He said the following:

To be successful, today's communications professional should be humble enough to realize that the power to persuade is very limited. Success in the 21st century comes from reading the public mind, not manipulating it. It follows that trust cannot be won by a single clever move, and certainly not by putting it in a mission statement or posting it on a Web site. It's not a quick fix. It's even more important to deliver trust programs week after week, and protecting your brand from folks who may have an axe to grind, especially on the all-too-available Internet.

Lee Levitt has, properly so, earned the moniker of veteran public relations practitioner. After serving many years in the front lines of PR, he has spent the past 20 years as a management consultant to PR firms. I asked Levitt what the future of public relations looks like to him. He said, "The profession has strengthened its position in society and has more to offer young people coming into the field today than ever before."

Bob Dilenschneider, you know already. He is very positive about the future and said the following:

> The impact and power of public relations has come into its own and the future of public relations, for someone who knows how to do it, is almost unlimited. There isn't an economic, legislative, or social decision made of any consequence today without taking public opinion into account.
>
> We have people who are making a difference when it comes to the advancement of cardiovascular research to the stock price of a company.
>
> Where does the talent come from? You look for the smartest people who can write and who have an ability to put one logical thought after another. If they come out of journalism, that's all the better. But it's not necessary.

THE INTERNET WILL GROW

The Internet and 24-hour cable television news is radically changing the newspaper business. In 2005, an item in the *Los Angeles Times* reported that hardened newspaper people have started eyeing public relations jobs they once would have disdained. They read daily about most newspapers cutting editorial staff.

Newspaper people across the country have descended into a "collective funk" over announcements of newsroom job cuts, according to the *Times*.

While newsrooms may be cutting back, don't fret; newspapers are going to be around for years to come. More and more of them are increasing their budgets for Internet operations. Newspapers are transferring their local marketplace dominance in print to online. Newspaper online revenues approached $4 billion in 2005.

More than 47 million people visited newspaper Web sites in the month of September 2005, the Audit Bureau of Circulation (ABC) tracked according to a *New York Times* article. That is almost one-third of all Internet users and is the highest number recorded since the ABC began tracking online usage in January 2004.

I predict the Internet will grow beyond our imaginations.

I asked Brian Pittman, the director of content for the Infocom Group, for his thoughts. With widely recognized brands in his stable like *Bulldog Reporter, PR University, Inside Health Media Daily Online Service, Media List Builder, PR Job Mart, the National PR Pitch Book Media Directories, the Daily 'Dog Online News Service,* and others, Pittman better have a handle on PR today and tomorrow. Pittman told me the following:

Make no bones about it, public relations is a work in progress. Staying relevant in today's ever-changing market is a moving target. Simply put, innovation has swept through the PR industry over the past ten years like a wireless tidal wave.

What's more, the pace is only going to quicken . . . and more changes are on the way. The choice is yours: You can either catch—or ride—that oncoming wave to success . . . or you can turn your back and get caught in the impact zone.

What do you need to know to survive?

Pittman told me the upshot is that survival—and success—in this field requires frontline practitioners, PR services, and observers alike to look to the horizon to know what's coming. Take, for example, the impact that blogs, podcasts, vidcasts, and other emerging tools are now having on the day-to-day outreach of public relations. Just five years ago, the mere mention of any of these—or even the concept of pitching an online influencer or brand evangelist—would have earned you little more than raised eyebrows.

Yet today, forward-thinking PR professionals all over the world consider these news tools (or an understanding of them) a fundamental part of the job—and so do their clients. That's because PR is a key ingredient of business survival these days, particularly because crises and attacks on your brand can break out overnight. Look no further than recent years that were filled with headlines of natural disasters, political turmoil, corporate humiliation, and the adverse economic trickle-down of situations like Enron and Martha Stewart . . . and you'll see it's true. According to Pittman:

> [S]avvy PR pros need to have tools on hand that aid in responding instantly to breaking news, emerging crises and challenges to the brand they've sworn to build, protect, and promote. Translation: It's no longer enough to craft a compelling release and clock out. That was yesterday.

I believe the do-it-yourselfer, the one-person PR shop, the advocate, and small-business professional can get in the game . . . but he and she must get with it. Pittman said the following:

It's no longer enough merely to "respond." Instead, the best of us must look ahead and learn to triangulate emerging trends, perceptions, and public behaviors . . . and to discern how these things impact the corporate goals of our employers—before they happen, take shape, or catch us by surprise. Again, it's all about looking ahead, watching for change on the horizon and turning into the wave instead of ducking and diving.

Tomorrow is here today. Believe it or not, some companies in the news-gathering field have started outsourcing journalism. Reuters, the financial news wire service, opened an office in India in 2005. The operation reports on companies' earnings, press releases, and filings with the U.S. Securities and Exchange Commission.

By outsourcing journalism and data processing, Reuters became the first large media company to base U.S. corporate-reporting functions offshore.

Outsourcing will grow in the years ahead. Because of my new computer and broadband Internet access, I had my share of tech support by telephone in 2005. As a foreign correspondent and consultant to Ferdinand Marcos, I spent a lot of time in the Philippines. Still, in 2005, I probably spent more time telephoning the Philippines (because of Dell computer tech support) in one month than I did in one year when I was involved in the area.

The public relations function in the future will be bigger than ever before not just for small businesses, but for big corporations as well. PR people will become much more important than advertising people, and will be essential in planning and policy direction. I also believe that executives with public relations backgrounds will be serving as chairpersons and CEOs of corporations that make all kinds of products and sell all kinds of services.

There is no fundamental reason why a PR professional should not head up IBM, General Electric, General Motors, or any advertising agency. Show me an ad agency with a PR pro at the helm, and I'll show you an ad agency looking to be number one. Perhaps if PR people had been in charge, GM and Ford would not have been hit as hard as they were in 2004, 2005, and 2006. The founders of Google, Amazon, and eBay truly were PR savvy, or they wouldn't have called their billion-dollar companies Google, Amazon, and eBay.

My statement about PR people running big companies might seem so exaggerated its preposterous. How could a PR practitioner ever hope to run an enterprise like GM?

Here is why I think it can happen. People who rise to the top of companies, big and small, all come from some specialized background. There is no such thing as an all-around executive who is equally trained in all disciplines and practices all disciplines to the same extent. No, you are a marketing manager, a financial manager, a production manager, an engineer, or whatever. Traditionally, the road to the top has been trod almost exclusively by line executives. For decades after the rise of large corporations, staff executives were virtually barred from leadership.

That has changed. Lawyers, research scientists, human resource managers—practitioners like these and other specialists can and do become CEOs of large organizations, although the bulk of these top jobs are still filled by persons from the conventional line backgrounds.

The point is that every CEO started as a specialist in something and then, after demonstrating broader management skills, was given greater responsibilities. It is reasonable to think that most top executives go about their jobs with approaches that have been shaped by their specialties. Marketing executives look at plans and decisions in terms of their effect on selling, financial people are keenly conscious of the money aspects of what is going on, and so on.

Advertising specialists do not become heads of giant companies. Powerful as it is, advertising is a sharply defined discipline that is devoted strictly to selling things through the use of paid-for time and space.

Some would argue that when the big advertising agencies started buying the big public relations agencies, they forced their ways on their new PR subsidiaries to the subsidiaries detriment. I repeat, PR people should head up the advertising conglomerates. Maybe then they wouldn't be on the receiving end of the wrath of the important trade media like the O'Dwyer newsletter.

Jack O'Dwyer believes the conglomerates are stifling the PR agencies they acquired in the last decade. O'Dwyer says:

> As far as we can see, every penny is being pinched by their PR wings, from agency events to individual lunches with the press, memberships in PR groups, and subscriptions to industry publications. Ketchum, for instance, cut its PRSA members from more than 80 in 2001 to about 30 in 2005.
>
> The smaller and midsize PR independents, which compete against these giants, are now seeing light at the end of the tunnel.
>
> They can verify their fee income and employment figures, something none of the big PR operations have been allowed to do since 2001.

Public relations, in its mature form, is a broader discipline than advertising. As the range of topics covered in this book indicates, public relations now penetrates a surprising number of important areas. It is a two-way discipline. Companies of the future will have well-rounded PR functions that provide input on all major moves the organization makes. It will be no different for the small businessman who is fast becoming PR savvy. And why not? The reaction of the public at large—and of all discrete publics—is a paramount consideration in most corporate planning and should be in small-business planning. The likely reactions of relevant publics—customers, communities, citizens, legislators, and others—will be probed and evaluated, not in a seat-of-the-pants fashion, but through an array of opinion-measuring techniques. This job will be done by public relations.

Had PR people been in charge of companies like Enron, WorldCom, Tyco, Adelphia Communications, and many more, our country might be in even better shape than it is today. And scores of investors would have more money in their bank accounts.

PR MOLDING POLICY

Before we have gone very far into the 21st century, public relations will be taken for granted as a major element in just about every corporation, organization, small business, cause, or local, regional, or national government agency, much like marketing, finance, and human resources. The work of PR practitioners will be influential and sometimes decisive in molding policy.

That being the case, there is no logical reason why executives who come out of the public relations discipline cannot run big companies just as well as executives who come out of the traditional mainstream disciplines. Indeed, it can be argued that someone who is gifted in the analysis and influencing of public opinion is a more likely choice to run a corporation or giant organization than an engineer or a lawyer.

"Insanity," you could say. You might talk to Bill Novelli, my former boss at the giant PR firm, Porter Novelli. When the advocacy group the American Association for Retired Persons (AARP) needed a chief executive officer to run its organization of more than 35 million members with billions of dollars in revenue from AARP-related programs, it didn't choose a financial wiz; it chose PR veteran Novelli. Under CEO Novelli, the *New York Times* reported in 2005, "AARP is acting a lot like a for-profit corporation these days."

Public relations practitioners have certain important qualifications for high corporate positions that are not necessarily possessed by other specialists. For one thing, PR professionals look realistically at what a company does and ask tough questions about it. Public relations practitioners cannot settle for inadequate answers, fuzzy explanations, or assumptions that a thing is OK because it has always been done a certain way. They have to be able to put things into plain language, so that reasonable people can understand them. The following is a good rule for CEOs and small-business people: If it cannot be explained, it should be fixed or abolished. Public relations professionals see a lot that is difficult, at best, to explain. As it stands now, they have to grit their teeth and make the best of it. Empowered as CEOs, they could change things.

Public relations literacy is spreading down to the grassroots level and new technology is allowing it to grow fast. The inexorable growth in the importance of public relations will make it a standard subject in any school's curriculum that prepares people for business or public service careers . . . if the schools find the teachers, that is. While more and more students are enrolling in PR classes, fewer and fewer people are available to teach them.

In the meantime, those who realize the crucial nature of public relations will have to seek PR literacy on their own.

This book is my contribution to that vital process.

Okay, you have gotten this far and I may have lost you in one of the previous chapters.

Perhaps you're the owner of that bead store I wrote about. You're still thinking PR is not for you. Tell yourself over and over again you can rise to the occasion. You may have to read one or more chapters again just as you did in school. Hey, how long did it take you to learn how to string beads?

Yet you still have a question and no one to turn to? Wrong. Help is on the way. I won't leave you out there dangling. In my lifetime I have probably faced every conceivable PR problem. Hopefully I can answer your question. Try me. Just e-mail me at *Lenpr@ bellsouth.net* and I will get back to you with an answer as soon as my schedule permits . . . free of charge, of course. I would also love to hear about your new successes in the mighty world of public relations.

This book is my contribution to the future; my thanks to you for buying this book and more thanks for reading it.

Good luck.

Leonard

Leonard Saffir is an award-winning public relations and journalism professional whose career also spans publishing, television, the Internet, and politics.

From 1984 through 1990, Saffir was executive vice president of Porter Novelli, one of the world's largest public relations firms. Saffir's duties included company management, new business development, and supervision of accounts in the areas of consumer products, crisis communications, sponsorships, litigation, film and television, entertainment, special events, marketing, and automotive.

For long-time client Philip Morris, Saffir developed and worked on numerous major projects in corporate image, sports, entertainment, music, and the arts. He played a major role in the highly successful Marlboro Country Music program; in Virginia Slims Women's Tennis; and led Marlboro into Indy Car auto racing. He created Porsche USA's first crisis communications plan and developed a technology-driven pressroom for the giant Detroit Auto Show for Michelin. Other former clients include MasterCard, Pepsi Cola, Bristol-Myers, Mattel, General Foods, Kraft, Amtrak, and Johnson & Johnson.

His work during litigation, representing the owner of the five-star La Mansion Hotel, San Antonio, versus Metropolitan Life Insurance Company, led to a settlement for his client of tens of millions of dollars and prompted his client's trial attorney to say publicly, "The lawyers didn't win this for Pat Kennedy, Len Saffir did."

Saffir is the author of *Power Public Relations, How to Get PR to Work for You,* hardcover, 1992; paperback, 1994. It was a main selection of the Executive Program book club. A second book,

Power Public Relations: How to Master the New PR, was published in January 2000 by McGraw-Hill. It was required reading by marketing and communications departments at many colleges and universities. McGraw-Hill published a Palm Digital Edition in 2002; Microsoft Reader and e-Books marketed an online edition.

Saffir was a founder of the *New York Standard,* an award-winning daily newspaper published during a 114-day newspaper strike that sold more than 25 million copies, carried 3 million lines of advertising, and showed a profit of several million dollars on some $10 million in revenue. He was a founder and publisher of the *Latin American Times,* an English daily newspaper praised by President Lyndon Johnson. He founded and served as publisher, editor-in-chief, and president of the *Trib,* New York's first new morning newspaper in 38 years and praised by Rupert Murdoch. Three former members of President Reagan's and President Ford's cabinets served on the company's board of directors. He was publisher and editor of *The Sun,* an award-winning weekly newspaper published in New York's Hamptons.

Saffir served in the U.S. Marine Corps as a public-information specialist. Following his military service, he was a U.S. and foreign correspondent for Hearst's International News Service in New York, Dallas, and Tokyo. He has written for many publications including the *New York Times, Washington Post, South Florida Sun-Sentinel, Miami Herald, Good Housekeeping Magazine,* and others. Saffir has received numerous journalism awards including the Sigma Delta Chi Professional Journalistic Society for distinguished journalistic achievement and awards and citations from the New York State Press Association and the Overseas Press Club of America. The Union League and Wharton Clubs of New York have honored him. Saffir is a past president of the Overseas Press Club of America, the nation's largest association of journalists engaged in foreign news reporting. He was assistant producer of a national one-hour Public Broadcasting System television special, *An Evening with Mark Twain.*

Saffir received the Public Relations Society of America's prestigious Silver Anvil and Big Apple awards and a PRSA Certificate of Commendation, and the Benjamin Franklin Award from the Chamber of Commerce & Industry of Northern New Jersey. He served for six years as chief of staff and press secretary to U.S. Senator James L. Buckley (R-NY) and was involved in all phases of the senator's work: legislative, political, and press. He traveled worldwide with Senator Buckley for meetings with foreign heads-of-state from Japan and Southeast Asia during the Vietnam War, to West and East Berlin, and to Russia during the cold war. Saffir has worked in numerous political campaigns in this country and abroad.

He has worked with Presidents Ford, Bush (the elder), and Reagan. He developed and implemented the strategy that led to Ferdinand Marcos's first election as president of the Philippines. Saffir was a key member of Buckley's winning campaign staff in 1970 and served as the senator's campaign manager in his 1976 campaign. He served as campaign manager in New York State Senator John Marchi's run for mayor of New York City.

Since relocating to Palm Beach County, Florida, in 1992, Saffir has been engaged in public relations consulting and writing. For two years he was an investigative reporter and columnist for a chain of Palm Beach County weekly newspapers. A major portion of his work has been picked up and posted on a nonprofit Web site.

Share the message!

Bulk discounts
Discounts start at only 10 copies and range from 30% to 55% off retail price based on quantity.

Custom publishing
Private label a cover with your organization's name and logo. Or, tailor information to your needs with a custom pamphlet that highlights specific chapters.

Ancillaries
Workshop outlines, videos, and other products are available on select titles.

Dynamic speakers
Engaging authors are available to share their expertise and insight at your event.

**Call Kaplan Publishing Corporate Sales at
1-800-621-9621, ext. 4444,
or e-mail kaplanpubsales@kaplan.com**